A Beginning Grammar of Classical and Hellenistic Greek

third revised edition
1991

Richard Cutter

BAYLOR UNIVERSITY PRESS

Third revised edition © 1991 by Baylor University Press, Waco, Texas 76798.
All Rights Reserved. No part of this publication may be reproduced, stored in a retrieval system, or transmitted, in any form or by any means, electronic, mechanical, photocopying, recording or otherwise, without the prior permission in writing of Baylor University Press.

First edition, published 1976
First revised edition, published 1981
Second revised edition, published 1985
Third revised edition, published 1991, reissued 2017

The ISBN for the 2017 reissue of the 1991 third revised edition is 978-1-4813-0912-7.

Contents

Chapter		Page
I	The Greek language. The Greek alphabet. Diphthongs. Iota subscript. Breathing marks. Punctuation.	1
II	Accent.	5
III	Inflection. First and second declension nouns.	7
IV	Continuation of first declension nouns. Articles. Adjectives.	12
V	Verbs. The present tense system.	19
VI	Future and aorist active indicative verbs.	25
VII	Perfect and pluperfect active indicative verbs. Dative of means. The objects of ἀκούω and πιστεύω.	31
VIII	Passive voice. Genitive of personal agent. Postpositives. Historical present.	37
IX	Middle voice. Deponent verbs. Context.	43
X	Personal pronouns. Declension of Ἰησοῦς. The article continued.	49
XI	Demonstrative, relative, reflexive, and reciprocal pronouns.	56
XII	Elision. Prepositions. Compound verbs. Adverbial and adjectival prepositional phrases.	63
XIII	Contract verbs. Possessive adjectives.	68
XIV	Dative of location. Indirect discourse. μι verbs.	73
XV	Reduplicated μι verbs.	78
XVI	μι verbs of the νυ class. Third declension nouns. Accusative of extent. Genitive of time.	84
XVII	More third declension nouns. Second aorist verbs with first aorist endings. Subject and predicate agreement.	90

XVIII	The adjectives πᾶς and ἀληθής. The indefinite pronoun τις. Numbers.	94
XIX	The interrogative pronoun τίς. Questions. Liquid verbs.	99
XX	The infinitive.	104
XXI	The present and future active participles. The attributive and substantival uses of the participle.	110
XXII	Aorist and perfect active participles. Circumstantial participles of time and cause.	115
XXIII	Middle voice of the participle. More circumstantial participles.	120
XXIV	Passive voice of the participle. Supplementary participles.	125
XXV	The imperative mood.	129
XXVI	The subjunctive mood in independent clauses.	135
XXVII	The subjunctive mood in dependent clauses. Conditional sentences.	140
XXVIII	Comparison of adjectives.	146
XXIX	The optative mood. Crasis. Conjunctions.	152
XXX	Verbal adjectives. Further uses of the cases.	158
	Appendix.	163

Chapter I

The Greek Language

The history of primitive Greek is obscure; however, it belongs to the ancient family of Indo-European languages which includes Albanian, Armenian, Balto-Slavic, Celtic, Germanic, Indo-Iranian, and Italic. At an early date Greek was divided into three dialects: Aeolic, Doric, and Ionic. The Ionic is particularly interesting to the student of Greek because Homer used this dialect.

The Attic dialect, a subsequent development of Ionic, gained pre-eminence over the other dialects. This was the language of Athens during the Classical period when Athens was the intellectual and cultural center of Greece. Aeschylus, Euripides, Thucydides, Xenophon, Plato, and Aristotle used this dialect.

Primarily due to Alexander's conquests in the fourth century before Christ, Attic Greek became the language of literature and commerce in the civilized world. Soon, however, people such as the merchants following Alexander's army, the soldiers themselves, and the citizens of the conquered countries made various changes in the Attic. This modified Greek is called the κοινὴ διάλεκτος, "the common dialect." Josephus, Polybius, Lucian, many of the Church Fathers, the translators of the Septuagint, and the writers of the New Testament used the κοινή.

Beginning in the middle of the sixth century and continuing until the middle of the fifteenth century, Constantinople was the center of Greek culture. The dialect of this period is called Byzantine Greek. The modern period is dated from the fall of Constantinople, 1453, to the present time. Thus, the Greek language has a continuous literary history of approximately 3000 years. The longevity of this language is truly amazing.* The Greek of today does differ from the Greek that Homer's characters used; however, when compared to the English language, this

---

* Of all the world's languages, Greek and the Latin-Romance group have the most complete unbroken record. Latin runs from approximately 500 B.C. to the end of the Roman Empire then merges with French in the 9th century and with Spanish and Italian in the 10th century. Written Greek should be dated sometime close to 1400 B.C., which is the approximate date of Linear B, a Minoan inscription.

difference is slight. An English speaker has difficulty with the English of Chaucer (14th century A.D.) and must treat the English of King Alfred (9th century A.D.) as a foreign tongue.

Greek Alphabet

Capitals	Small	Name	Pronunciation
Α	α	alpha	a as in father
Β	β	beta	
Γ	γ	gamma	g as in garage
Δ	δ	delta	
Ε	ε	epsilon	e as in set
Ζ	ζ	zeta	dz as in suds
Η	η	eta	e as in obey
Θ	θ	theta	th as in thin
Ι	ι	iota	i as in pit (short)
			i as in machine (long)
Κ	κ	kappa	
Λ	λ	lambda	
Μ	μ	mu	
Ν	ν	nu	
Ξ	ξ	xi	ks as in relax
Ο	ο	omikron	o as in pot
Π	π	pi	
Ρ	ρ	rho	
Σ	σ, ς	sigma	
Τ	τ	tau	
Υ	υ	upsilon	u as in cute
Φ	φ	phi	ph as in phone
Χ	χ	chi	ch as in chemistry
Ψ	ψ	psi	ps as in tipsy
Ω	ω	omega	o as in obey

Capital letters are not used as frequently in Greek as in English; therefore, the student should first memorize the small letters. Capital letters are used at the beginning of a paragraph, at the beginning of a direct quotation, and as the first letter of a proper name.

Letters vary in size, and comparative terminology is used to describe them. That is, alpha is on an imaginary line; beta is on, below, and above this line; gamma is on and below; delta is on and above this line: α β γ δ. α, ε, ι, κ, ν, ο, π, σ, τ, υ, and ω are written on the line. β, ζ, ξ, φ, and ψ are written on, above, and below the line. γ, η, μ, ρ, ς, and χ are written on and below the line. δ, θ, and λ are written on and above the line.

The letter "γ" is pronounced like the English "n" when it precedes κ, χ, ξ, or another γ; for example, ἄγγελος is an/gel/os.

The vowels "ε" and "o" are always short, while "η" and "ω" are always long. α, ι, and υ may be either long or short.

Diphthongs

A diphthong is a combination of two vowels in one syllable. There are seven diphthongs:

>αι pronounced like "ai" in aisle
>ει pronounced like "a" in mate
>οι pronounced like "oi" in oil
>αυ pronounced like "au" in kraut
>ευ pronounced like "eu" in euphony
>ου pronounced like "oo" in moon
>υι pronounced like the word "we"

Diphthongs are always long except when αι and οι are the final letters in a word; that is, in λόγοις "οι" is long but in λόγοι "οι" is short.

A diaresis mark (¨) over the second vowel of two vowels which are normally a diphthong indicates that the two vowels are separate and not a diphthong; for example, ἀϊδνός has three syllables α/ιδ/νος, but αἴρω has two αι/ρω.

Iota Subscript

An iota is sometimes joined to a long α, η, or ω and carried as a subscript (ᾳ, ῃ, ῳ). The iota subscript is mute; thus the vowel with the subscript has its normal pronunciation.

Breathing Marks

The first syllable of a word beginning with a vowel or diphthong has a breathing mark. The rough breathing mark (῾) signifies that the word is pronounced with an "h" sound; for example, ἑν is pronounced "hen." A smooth breathing mark (᾿) does not affect the pronunciation of its vowel: ἐν is pronounced "en." When a word begins with a "ρ," the word has rough breathing: ῥῆμα. If a word begins with a diphthong, the second vowel has the breathing mark: αἴρω.

Punctuation

Greek has four marks of punctuation.* The comma (,) and the period (.) are the same as in English. The Greek colon (·) takes the place of the English colon and semicolon. The question mark (;) looks like the English semicolon.

---

* The paragraph was the most important punctuation in classical and κοινή Greek. Words were usually run together; however, some stop symbols, which differ from today's punctuation, were used sparingly. The question mark was not used until approximately 900 A. D. In fact, it is difficult to determine how much punctuation the writer of ancient Greek used (if indeed he used any). Editors and textual critics are responsible for the majority of the punctuation appearing in the printed texts of ancient Greek literature; this includes the New Testament.

The earliest Greek appeared in Homeric times and was called **boustrophedon**, or "as the ox plows." The first line reads from left to right, the next line reads from right to left, and so forth.

Chapter II

Accent

The least portion of writing or speech is a syllable. A Greek word has as many syllables as it has vowels or diphthongs. There is no rule to govern the dividing of a word into syllables. Therefore, the word λόγος could be divided λο-γος or λογ-ος. The important fact to note is that this word has two vowels; consequently, it has two syllables.

The last syllable of a word is the ultima, the next to last is the penult, and the syllable preceding the penult is the antepenult. Hence, in the word ἀπόστολος the ultima is --λος, the penult is --το--, the antepenult is --πος--, and in this word the first syllable (α--) has no name. Accent marks can only stand over the antepenult, penult, or ultima.

The length of a syllable is the same as the length of its vowel or diphthong. It is impossible to accent a word without knowing the length of its syllables.

There are three accent marks: acute (´), grave (`), and circumflex (ˆ). These marks originally indicated different pitches of the voice, but now they only indicate that their syllable is stressed. When a syllable has both the breathing and accent marks, the acute and grave are placed after the breathing mark; for example, αἴρω and ἕν. The circumflex stands over the breathing mark: οἶκος.

There are two questions that must be answered when accenting a word. First, which syllable is accented? Second, which accent mark is used? The following list of accent rules should be memorized.

Place of accent for verbs:
1. When the ultima is short, accent the antepenult; if there is no antepenult, accent the penult.
2. When the ultima is long, accent the penult.

<u>Place of accent for nouns</u>:
1. When the nominative singular has accent on the antepenult, it stays there. However, if the ultima becomes long, accent then moves to the penult.
2. When the nominative singular has accent on the penult or the ultima, it stays there.

<u>Kind of accent for verbs and nouns</u>:
The accent is always an acute with the following exceptions:
1. When the ultima is short, the accent on a long penult is a circumflex.
2. The accent on a long ultima may be a circumflex.
3. In a sentence a grave replaces the acute on the ultima when another word follows without intervening punctuation.

There are certain additions and modifications that must be made to these rules in future lessons.

Exercise

I. Accent the following noun forms whose nominative singulars are

θεός, τοῖχος, and ἀπόστολος.

1. θεον, θεε, θεοι, θεοις.

2. τοιχῳ, τοιχου, τοιχοι, τοιχοις.

3. αποστολοι, αποστολον, αποστολοις, αποστολε.

4. τοιχον, αποστολων, θεου.

II. Accent the following verb forms of λύω. The "υ" in each of the forms of λύω is long. When either an "α" or an "ι" is the final letter, it is short.

1. ἐλυομεν, λυε, λυετω.

2. λελυμεθα, ἐλυετε, λυσαι.

3. ἐλυου, λυουσι, ἐλυομην.

4. λυσον, ἐλυον, λυσομαι.

III. Pronounce each form in exercises I and II.

Chapter III

Inflection

First and Second Declension Nouns

Inflection

A language that changes the spelling of certain parts of speech to indicate their function in a sentence is an inflected language. Nouns, pronouns, adjectives, and verbs are inflected in Greek. Inflecting a noun, pronoun, or adjective is called declining. Inflecting a verb is conjugating. A noun is the name of a person, place, or thing; it has gender, case, and number.

Gender

The gender of a Greek noun is a matter of lexical study. In the English language a noun follows the natural order; thus, the names of males are masculine, those of females are feminine, and those of things are neuter. However, this is not true for the Greek language; for example, the word for house may be masculine or feminine, a church feminine, and a child neuter.

Number

Nouns may be singular, plural, or dual. The dual number occurs quite often in Homer, not too frequently in Attic Greek, and not at all in the New Testament. Therefore, the dual forms are only given in the appendix.

Case

There are five cases:
1. The nominative is the case of the subject of a verb;
2. The genitive is the case of possession or qualification, often expressed in English by using the preposition "of";

3. The <u>dative</u> is the case of the indirect object, often expressed by "to" or "for";
4. The <u>accusative</u> is the case of the direct object of a verb;
5. The <u>vocative</u> is the case of direct address.

This is not a comprehensive list of the uses of each case, and in future chapters new uses will be discussed.

Declensions

The English noun shows its case by the use of prepositions or by its position in a sentence. The spelling of a Greek noun shows its case. There are three declensions; γραφή and εἰρήνη are illustrations of feminine nouns of the first declension.

	Singular	
Nom. & Voc.	γραφή	εἰρήνη
Gen.	γραφῆς	εἰρήνης
Dat.	γραφῇ	εἰρήνῃ
Acc.	γραφήν	εἰρήνην
	Plural	
Nom. & Voc.	γραφαί	εἰρῆναι
Gen.	γραφῶν	εἰρηνῶν
Dat.	γραφαῖς	εἰρήναις
Acc.	γραφάς	εἰρήνας

Observe:
1. In each form of γραφή and εἰρήνη there is a portion of the word (γραφ and εἰρην) that does not change; this is the noun stem.
2. When the ultima is accented, the genitives and datives have the circumflex; the other cases have the acute.
3. The genitive plural has a circumflex on the ultima regardless of the accent on the nominative singular.
4. The "α" of the accusative plural is always long.
5. All feminine nouns whose nominative singulars end with an "η" and genitive singulars end with an ης are first declension nouns and are declined like γραφή and εἰρήνη.

The feminine noun ἔρημος, the masculine noun οἶκος, and the neuter noun ἱερόν illustrate the second declension.

Singular

Nom.	ἔρημος	οἶκος	ἱερόν
Gen.	ἐρήμου	οἴκου	ἱεροῦ
Dat.	ἐρήμῳ	οἴκῳ	ἱερῷ
Acc.	ἔρημον	οἶκον	ἱερόν
Voc.	ἔρημε	οἶκε	ἱερόν

Plural

Nom. & Voc.	ἔρημοι	οἶκοι	ἱερά
Gen.	ἐρήμων	οἴκων	ἱερῶν
Dat.	ἐρήμοις	οἴκοις	ἱεροῖς
Acc.	ἐρήμους	οἴκους	ἱερά

Observe:
1. Second declension nouns, like the first declension, use the circumflex on the genitives and datives when the ultima is accented.
2. The feminine and masculine genders are declined identically.
3. The nominative, accusative, and vocative singulars of the neuter noun have the same form. The nominative, accusative, and vocative plurals of the neuter also have the same form (a short "α").
4. The ultima of the genitive plural is not accented unless the nominative singular is.
5. All feminine and masculine nouns whose nominative singular endings are ος and genitive singulars are ου are second declension nouns and are declined like ἔρημος and οἶκος. All neuter nouns whose nominative and genitive singular endings are ον and ου, respectively, are second declension and declined like ἱερόν.

Vocabulary

Learn the following:

1. ἄνθρωπος, ου, ὁ	man	(anthropology)
2. ἀπόστολος, ου, ὁ	apostle	(apostle)
3. γραφή, ῆς, ἡ	writing	(graphite)
4. δῶρον, ου, τό	gift	(Dorothy)
5. εἰρήνη, ης, ἡ	peace	(Irene)

6. ἔρημος, ου, ἡ	wilderness or desert	(hermit)
7. ζωή, ῆς, ἡ	life	(zoology)
8. ἱερόν, οῦ, τό	temple	(hierarchy)
9. ὁδός, οῦ, ἡ	road or way	(anode)
10. οἶκος, ου, ὁ	house	(economy)
11. παραβολή, ῆς, ἡ	parable	(parable)
12. υἱός, οῦ, ὁ	son	
13. φωνή, ῆς, ἡ	voice	(phonograph)
14. ψυχή, ῆς, ἡ	life or soul*	(psychology)

It is important to study the information given with each vocabulary word. The first word is listed: ἄνθρωπος, ου, ὁ man (anthropology). "ἄνθρωπος" is the nominative singular and is called the vocabulary form. "ου" is the genitive singular ending. "ὁ" is the masculine article and it indicates that ἄνθρωπος is a masculine noun. "Man" is the English translation for ἄνθρωπος. "(anthropology)" is an English derivative of the Greek word and is given only to aid in memorizing. Not all Greek words have English derivatives; however, 13% of the English language is derived from the Greek.

Translation
<u>Translate (accent and pronounce)</u>:

1. Of an apostle   Of apostles
2. For sons   Of a son
3. Voices (acc.)   Voice (acc.)
4. Of lives   For a life
5. For peace   Peace (gen. pl.)
6. For roads   For houses
7. For parables   To parables
8. Temples (acc.)   Temples (nom.)

---

* Two definitions are given for ψυχή; moreover, there are other definitions such as "breath," mind," and "appetite," that could have been given. A large number of the vocabulary words in this grammar have definitions that are not given. The purpose and length of a beginning grammar does not permit a comprehensive listing of all the meanings of the vocabulary words.

The words that are chosen for the vocabulary in this grammar are chosen because they occur most frequently in the New Testament. This selection also gives a basic vocabulary for classical Greek. Of 4829 words in the New Testament (not counting proper nouns), 3933 belong to classical while 966 are later or foreign words.

9. Of houses   Houses (nom.)
10. Gift (acc.)   Of a gift
11. Souls (nom.)   For souls
12. For writing   Writings (acc.)
13. Men (voc.)   Man (voc.)
14. Of a desert   Of a wilderness

Translate the boldfaced words:

Luke 10:6 ἐὰν ἐκεῖ ᾖ **υἱὸς εἰρήνης**, If _____ _____ were there.

Matt. 2:11 προσήνεγκαν αὐτῷ **δῶρα**, They brought to him _____.

Acts 5:4 οὐκ ἐψεύσω **ἀνθρώποις**. You have not lied _____.

Luke 12:14 **Ἄνθρωπε**, Τίς με κατέστησεν; "_____, who appointed me?"

Chapter IV

A Continuation of First Declension Nouns
Articles
Adjectives

A Continuation of First Declension Nouns

The vowels "α" and "η" are closely related; therefore, it is not surprising that the "α" rather than the "η" is sometimes used in the case endings of the first declension. The feminine nouns δόξα and ἡμέρα are declined as follows:

Singular

Nom. & Voc.	δόξα	ἡμέρα
Gen.	δόξης	ἡμέρας
Dat.	δόξῃ	ἡμέρᾳ
Acc.	δόξαν	ἡμέραν

Plural

Nom. & Voc.	δόξαι	ἡμέραι
Gen.	δοξῶν	ἡμερῶν
Dat.	δόξαις	ἡέραις
Acc.	δόξας	ἡμέρας

When the vocabulary form of a first declension feminine noun ends with an "α," and the last letter of the noun stem is ε, ι, or ρ, it is declined like ἡμέρα. If the vocabulary form ends in an "α" and the last letter of the stem is not an ε, ι, or ρ, it is declined like δόξα; the genitive singular ending is ης and the dative singular is "ῃ."*

Masculine nouns of the first declension differ from the feminine in the nominative, genitive, and vocative singulars.

---

* In the appendix see ἀλήθεια. All nouns of the first declension that have the acute on the antepenult of the nominative singular have the acute on the antepenult of the accusative singular.

12

	Singular	
Nom.	νεανίας	προφήτης
Gen.	νεανίου	προφήτου
Dat.	νεανίᾳ	προφήτῃ
Acc.	νεανίαν	προφήτην
Voc.	νεανία	προφῆτα
	Plural	
Nom. & Voc.	νεανίαι	προφῆται
Gen.	νεανιῶν	προφητῶν
Dat.	νεανίαις	προφήταις
Acc.	νεανίας	προφήτας

The differences between the declensions of νεανίας and προφήτης are a result of the "ε, ι, and ρ" rule. Moreover, it should be observed that the plural case endings of all first declension nouns are identical.

Articles

Indefinite Articles

In English the indefinite articles, "a" and "an," designate an object as merely one of a general class or kind. There is no indefinite article in Greek; but when the definite article does not modify a substantive* (particularly a concrete substantive), an indefinite article may be used in the English translation.

The Definite Article

The definite article points out one or more particular objects as distinct from others of the same kind. It is declined as follows:

	Singular		
	Mas.	Fem.	Neuter
Nom.	ὁ	ἡ	τό
Gen.	τοῦ	τῆς	τοῦ
Dat.	τῷ	τῇ	τῷ
Acc.	τόν	τήν	τό

---

* A substantive is a noun or noun equivalent.

Plural

	Mas.	Fem.	Neuter
Nom.	οἱ	αἱ	τά
Gen.	τῶν	τῶν	τῶν
Dat.	τοῖς	ταῖς	τοῖς
Acc.	τούς	τάς	τά

The masculine and feminine nominatives of both numbers are proclitics. A proclitic is a word that goes so closely with the followng word that it has no accent.

For the time being, the presence or absence of the definite article should be indicated in English translations.

καὶ ἦν ἐκεῖ ἄνθρωπος (Mark 3:1); "And a man was there."

καὶ λέγει τῷ ἀνθρώπῳ (Mark 3:3); "And he spoke to **the** man."

Adjectives

An adjective is a word that describes or limits a substantive. The substantive governs the case, gender, and number of the modifying adjective. The declensions of the adjectives ἀγαθός and ἅγιος are as follows:

Singular

	Mas.	Fem.	Neuter	Mas.	Fem.	Neuter
Nom.	ἀγαθός	ἀγαθή	ἀγαθόν	ἅγιος	ἁγία	ἅγιον
Gen.	ἀγαθοῦ	ἀγαθῆς	ἀγαθοῦ	ἁγίου	ἁγίας	ἁγίου
Dat.	ἀγαθῷ	ἀγαθῇ	ἀγαθῷ	ἁγίῳ	ἁγίᾳ	ἁγίῳ
Acc.	ἀγαθόν	ἀγαθήν	ἀγαθόν	ἅγιον	ἁγίαν	ἅγιον
Voc.	ἀγαθέ	ἀγαθή	ἀγαθόν	ἅγιε	ἁγία	ἅγιον

Plural

	Mas.	Fem.	Neuter	Mas.	Fem.	Neuter
N. & V.	ἀγαθοί	ἀγαθαί	ἀγαθά	ἅγιοι	ἅγιαι	ἅγια
Gen.	ἀγαθῶν	ἀγαθῶν	ἀγαθῶν	ἁγίων	ἁγίων	ἁγίων
Dat.	ἀγαθοῖς	ἀγαθαῖς	ἀγαθοῖς	ἁγίοις	ἁγίαις	ἁγίοις
Acc.	ἀγαθούς	ἀγαθάς	ἀγαθά	ἁγίους	ἁγίας	ἅγια

Observe:

1. ἅγιος illustrates that the "ε, ι, ρ" rule also applies to adjectives.
2. The "α" in the endings of ἅγιος for the nominative, accusative, and vocative feminine singulars is long. This is true of all adjectives whose stems end with an ε, ι, or ρ.

3. The ultima of the genitive feminine plural is accented only when the ultima of the nominative singular is accented.
4. Since the declension of ἀγαθός follows the declension of first and second declension nouns, a review of the declension of ἀγαθός is a review of the declensions of nouns.

In the vocabulary ἀγαθός is listed: ἀγαθός, ή, όν   good. "η" is the abbreviation for the nominative feminine singular, ἀγαθή; "ov" is the abbreviation for the nominative neuter singular, ἀγαθόν; "good" is the vocabulary meaning. A few adjectives have "o" rather than "ov" for their endings in the neuter singular of the nominative, accusative, and vocative cases; see ἄλλος, η, ο.

Attributive and Predicate Adjectives

An adjective modifies a substantive in the attributive position when the adjective has the definite article; the substantive may or may not have the article. This construction indicates that the adjective gives an attribute of the substantive. In the following examples ἀγαθός is in the attributive position:

ὁ ἀγαθὸς ἄνθρωπος
ὁ ἀγαθὸς ὁ ἄνθρωπος
ὁ ἄνθρωπος ὁ ἀγαθός.

Each of the above sentence fragments is translated "the good man."

An adjective is in the predicate position with a substantive when the substantive has the article and the adjective does not. In this construction the adjective makes a predication about the substantive. The following examples, both translated "The man is good," are complete sentences.

ὁ ἄνθρωπος ἀγαθός.
ἀγαθὸς ὁ ἄνθρωπος.

Observe the following examples:

ἄξιος (ἄξιος, α, ον, worthy) ὁ ἐργάτης (ἐργάτης, ου, ὁ, workman) (Matt. 10:10); "The workman is worthy."

παθητὸς (παθητός, ή, όν, capable of suffering) ὁ Χριστός (Χριστός, οῦ, ὁ, Christ); (Acts 26:23) "Christ is capable of suffering."

An adjective may modify a noun without an article:

ἀγαθὸς ἄνθρωπος

Since the use or disuse of the definite article indicates the position of the adjective, the context must show whether ἀγαθὸς ἄνθρωπος is to be translated "a good man" or "A man is good."

Substantival Use

Adjectives may function as substantives.* The gender and number of the adjective should be reflected in the translations:

ὁ ἀγαθός	"the good man"
ἡ ἀγαθή	"the good woman"
τὸ ἀγαθόν	"the good thing"
οἱ ἀγαθοί	"the good men"
αἱ ἀγαθαί	"the good women"
τὰ ἀγαθά	"the good things".

Vocabulary

1. ἀγαθός, ή, όν — good — (agathism)
2. ἀγάπη, ης, ἡ — love
3. ἅγιος, α, ον — holy — (Hagiographa)
4. ἀλήθεια, ας, ἡ — truth — (alethiology)
5. ἄλλος, η, ο — other or another — (allegory)
6. δόξα, ης, ἡ — glory — (doxology)
7. ἐκκλησία, ας, ἡ — church — (ecclesiastic)
8. ἡμέρα, ας, ἡ — day — (ephemeral)
9. θάνατος, ου, ὁ — death — (*Thanatopsis*)
10. θεός, οῦ, ὁ — God — (theology)
11. καλός, ή, όν — beautiful or good — (kaleidoscope)
12. μαθητής, οῦ, ὁ — disciple — (mathematics)
13. νεανίας, ου, ὁ — young man — (neophyte)
14. νεκρός, ά, όν — dead — (necropolis)
15. νόμος, ου, ὁ — law — (Deuteronomy)
16. ὁ, ἡ, τό — the
17. ὄχλος, ου, ὁ — crowd — (ochlophobia)
18. προφήτης, ου, ὁ — prophet — (prophet)

---

* Greek is not the only language that uses adjectives substantively. Alan Moorehead in *No Room in the Ark*, pp. 145-146, states that in a part of Africa cattle are so important that if an adjective stands by itself, the noun it qualifies is always understood to be a cow.

Translation

1. The disciples are dead to the law.
2. The other parable is beautiful for the apostle.
3. The way of peace is good for a church.
4. Is the holy temple beautiful?
5. The good young man of the holy law is holy.
6. ἡ φωνὴ τῆς ἀληθείας ἁγία ἀνθρώποις ἐξουσίας (ἐξουσία, ας, ἡ, authority).
7. ταῖς ἰσχυραῖς (ἰσχυρός, ά, όν, strong) ἡ ἀγαθὴ ὁδὸς ἀγάπης ἁγία.
8. νεκρὰ ἡ ἐκκλησία ἡ ἄλλη τῷ ἀδελφῷ (ἀδελφός, οῦ, ὁ, brother) τοῦ νέου (νέος, α, ον, new) ἀποστόλου.
9. τοῖς ἄλλοις μαθηταῖς ἡ ἡμέρα κακῆς (κακός, ή, όν, evil) δόξης καλή.
10. αἱ ἄλλαι ἔρημοι τῆς ἐμῆς (ἐμός, ή, όν, my) βασιλείας (βασιλεία, ας, ἡ, kingdom) καλαί;
11. ἀγαθὰ τὰ δῶρα προφήτου ταῖς ἐκκλησίαις τῶν πρώτων (πρῶτος, η, ον, first) διδασκάλων (διδάσκαλος, ου, ὁ, teacher).
12. αἱ ἀγαθαὶ καλαί· νεκραὶ αἱ ἄλλαι.
13. ἅγια τὰ καλὰ τοῦ θεοῦ τοῖς υἱοῖς τοῦ νεκροῦ;
14. ἡ ἡμέρα θανάτου καλὴ τοῖς ἀγαθοῖς υἱοῖς τοῦ ἄλλου τοῦ προφήτου.

Matt. 5:9

μακάριοι (μακάριος, α, ον, blessed) οἱ εἰρηνοποιοί (εἰρηνοποιός, οῦ, ὁ, peacemaker).

Rom. 7:12

ἡ ἐντολὴ (ἐντολή, ῆς, ἡ, commandment) ἁγία καὶ (and) δικαία (δίκαιος, α, ον, just) καὶ ἀγαθή.

Matt. 13:48

συνέλεξαν (they gathered) τὰ καλὰ εἰς (into) ἄγγη (containers).

Luke 7:15

ἀνεκαθίσεν (sat up) ὁ νεκρός.

Chapter V

Verbs

The Present Tense System

Introduction
A verb is a word that expresses action, being, or state of being. A Greek verb has tense, voice, mood, number, and person.

Tense
Tense is that quality of a verb which expresses the time and kind of action.

Voice
Voice is the quality of a verb which points out the relation of the subject to the action. The active voice shows that the subject does the action, and the passive voice shows that the subject receives the action. Unlike English, Greek has a middle voice which will be discussed in a future chapter.

Mood
The mood of a verb indicates the relation of the action to reality. The indicative mood tells that the relation is positive. The other moods will be discussed in future chapters.

Number
Number is that quality of a verb which specifies whether it is singular or plural. Like the noun, the verb may have dual number in classical Greek; however, the dual number is used so infrequently that its verb forms are included only in the appendix.

Person

Person is the quality of a verb that points out whether the subject is speaking, being spoken to, or being spoken about.

Principal Parts

The leading inflected forms of a verb are called principal parts. From these forms all other verb forms are derived. In English the principal parts are the present infinitive, the past tense, and the past participle: drive, drove, driven. In Greek the principal parts are the present, the future, the aorist, the perfect active, the perfect middle, and the aorist passive: λύω, λύσω, ἔλυσα, λέλυκα, λέλυμαι, ἐλύθην.

Imperfect and Present Active Indicatives

The first of the principal parts of the Greek verb meaning "liberate" is λύω. The present tense stem is obtained by dropping the "ω." On this tense stem, λυ, all forms of the present tense system are formed. The present and the imperfect actives are conjugated as follows:

	Present Active Indicative		Imperfect Active Indicative	
	S.	Pl.	S.	Pl.
1.	λύω	λύομεν	ἔλυον	ἐλύομεν
2.	λύεις	λύετε	ἔλυες	ἐλύετε
3.	λύει	λύουσι (ν)	ἔλυε (ν)	ἔλυον

The present tense stem of the other verbs listed in the vocabulary of this chapter may also be found by dropping the "ω" in the vocabulary form. Thus, the present tense stem of βλέπω is βλεπ. βλέπω is conjugated by suffixing the same endings that are used with λύω.

	Present Active Indicative		Imperfect Active Indicative	
	S.	Pl.	S.	Pl.
1.	βλέπω	βλέπομεν	ἔβλεπον	ἐβλέπομεν
2.	βλέπεις	βλέπετε	ἔβλεπες	ἐβλέπετε
3.	βλέπει	βλέπουσι (ν)	ἔβλεπε (ν)	ἔβλεπον

Personal Endings

The suffixes joined to the tense stem to give voice, number, and person are called personal endings. The primary* active endings are ω, εις, ει, μεν, τε, and ουσι. The secondary endings are ν, ς, -, μεν, τε, and ν.

Variable Vowels

The vowel which is used between the tense stem and the personal ending is called the variable vowel. It is an "o" before either a "μ" or "ν," and an "ε" before other letters. In the imperfect active conjugations of λύω and βλέπω, the variable vowels are easily seen; however, since the variable vowels in the third plural and in all the singular forms of the present active conjugation have contracted with the personal endings, the "ε" and "o" are not as discernable as in the imperfect conjugation.

Augments

In addition to using the secondary endings to indicate past time, Greek also uses an augment. When a verb begins with a consonant, the augment is an "ε" prefixed to the verb stem: the imperfect of λύω is ἔλυον. When the stem of a verb begins with a vowel, the augment usually causes a lengthening of the initial vowel: the imperfect of ἀκούω is ἤκουον; ἐσθίω is ἤσθιον; ὀφείλω is ὤφειλον. Except for the augmenting, the imperfect active conjugations of these verbs are the same as for the verbs starting with consonants. Observe the following conjugation of ἀκούω:

Imperfect Active Indicative

	Singular	Plural
1.	ἤκουον	ἠκούομεν
2.	ἤκουες	ἠκούετε
3.	ἤκουε (ν)	ἤκουον

Movable ν

The letter "ν" is frequently suffixed to third person singular verbs ending in "ε" (ἔλυεν), and to words ending in σι (λύουσιν). This consonant is called a movable

---

* The primary tenses are the future, perfect, and the present. The secondary tenses are the imperfect, aorist, and pluperfect.

"ν" and is added for euphony only. In classical Greek it was used before words beginning with a vowel and at the end of a clause. However, the writers of κοινή Greek did not strictly adhere to this pattern:

καὶ ἐκήρυσσεν λέγων, Mark 1:7.

Subject and Verb Agreement

When a personal pronoun is the subject of a clause, the personal ending of the verb indicates the subject: σοι λέγω (Mark 2:11), "I speak to you"; λέγουσι αὐτῷ (Mark 1:30), "**They** speak to him." When there is an external subject, it must agree with the verb in person and number: οἱ ἀδελφοὶ βλέπουσι, "The brothers see"; or ὁ ἀδελφὸς βλέπει, "The brother sees." If the subject of the clause is a neuter plural, the verb may have singular number. Both of the following sentences are correct:

τὰ τέκνα βλέπουσι.
τὰ τέκνα βλέπει.

Each is translated "The children see." Observe the neuter plural subjects in the following sentences:

τὰ **πρόβατα** τῆς φωνῆς (the object of ἀκούει) αὐτοῦ (his) **ἀκούει**
(John 10:3); "The **sheep hear** his voice."
οὐκ **ἤκουσαν** (1st aorist active indicative 3rd person plural) αὐτῶν (object of ἤκουσαν "them") τὰ **πρόβατα** (John 10:8); "The **sheep** did not **hear** them."

Translation of the Tenses

The present indicative may indicate progressive or simple action in present time; thus, λύω is translated either "I am liberating" or "I liberate." The imperfect indicative indicates progressive action in past time; thus, ἔλυον is translated "I was liberating."

Negatives

The negative adverb used with the indicative verb is οὐ. It is spelled οὐκ before words beginning with a vowel and having smooth breathing. Before words beginning with a vowel which have rough breathing, the negative is spelled οὐχ.*

---

* In conversation the ancient Greeks used a downward nod of the head to indicate "yes," and an upward nod to indicate "no."

Vocabulary

1.	ἀδελφός, οῦ, ὁ	brother	(Philadelphia)
2.	ἀκούω	hear	(acoustics)
3.	ἁμαρτία, ας, ἡ	sin	(hamartiology)
4.	βλέπω	see	(ablepsy)
5.	γιγνώσκω or γινώσκω	know	(diagnosis)
6.	διδάσκω	teach	(didactic)
7.	ἐξουσία, ας, ἡ	authority	
8.	καί, conjunction	and	
9.	κύριος, ου, ὁ	Lord, master, or sir	
10.	λαμβάνω	take or receive	(epilepsy)
11.	λόγος, ου, ὁ	word	(logic)
12.	λύω	liberate or destroy	(paralysis)
13.	ὅλος, η, ον	whole	(holocaust)
14.	οὐ, οὐκ, οὐχ	no	(utopia)
15.	οὐρανός, οῦ, ὁ	heaven	(uranium)
16.	πιστεύω	believe or trust [takes the dative]	(pistology)
17.	πρῶτος, η, ον	first	(prototype)
18.	ὥρα, ας, ἡ	hour	(horoscope)

Translation

1. The good brothers are seeing the sins of the disciple's church.
2. The first woman was not receiving the beautiful gifts of love.
3. Does the apostle of the dead prophet trust the words of peace?
4. The temples of the god are receiving the first gifts for the gods.
5. We know the holy authority of the beautiful heaven, and you were teaching the other words to the good young men.
6. ἐπίστευον τῷ πρώτῳ λόγῳ τοῦ μαθητοῦ οἱ ἄλλοι οἱ ἀδελφοί.
7. τὰς καλὰς τῆς ἄλλης τῆς ἐκκλησίας οὐκ ἀκούεις τῷ ἀποστόλῳ.
8. οἱ πρῶτοι μαθηταὶ τῷ ἁγίῳ θεῷ διδάσκουσιν ἀνθρώπους ἁμαρτίας;

9. ἤγγελλον (ἀγγέλλω, announce) τοὺς ἀγαθοὺς τοὺς λόγους ἀληθείας.
10. ἀγαθὸς ὁ ὅλος λόγος ἁγίου κυρίου ποιητῇ (ποιητής, οῦ, ὁ, poet).
11. ἔβλεπεν τὰ ἱερὰ τοῦ καλοῦ τοῦ κυρίου τὴν ἐξουσίαν τῆς ὥρας.
12. λύω τῷ θεῷ τοὺς προφήτας τοῦ καλοῦ ἱεροῦ καὶ πιστεύουσι τῷ θεῷ.
13. τοὺς νόμους οὐρανοῦ γιγνώσκομεν· τὰ ἀγαθὰ ἀγάπης οὐκ ἐγινώσκετε.
14. γιγνώσκουσιν οἱ ἀδελφοὶ τοῦ νεανίου τὴν ἀγαθὴν ὁδὸν τῆς ψυχῆς;
15. ἡ νεκρὰ ἐκκλησία τοὺς λόγους ζωῆς οὐκ ἐλάμβανε καὶ διδάσκει τὸν ὄχλον ἁμαρτίας τὰ τέκνα (τέκνον, ου, τό, child) τῆς ἐκκλησίας.

James 2:19
τὰ δαιμόνια (δαιμόνιον, ου, τό, demon) πιστεύουσιν καί φρίσσουσιν (φρίσσω, tremble).

II Cor. 12:14
οὐ γὰρ (for) ὀφείλει (ὀφείλω, ought) τὰ τέκνα (τέκνον, ου, τό, child) τοῖς γονεῦσιν (for parents) θησαυρίζειν (to save).

Acts 26:27
πιστεύεις, βασιλεῦ (king, vocative case) Ἀγρίππα (Agrippa, vocative case), τοῖς προφήταις;

Matt. 27:42
καταβάτω (come down) νῦν (now) ἀπὸ (from) τοῦ σταυροῦ (cross) καὶ πιστεύσομεν (fut. act. ind. 1 pl.) ἐπ' (upon) αὐτόν (him).

Chapter VI

Future and Aorist Active Indicative Verbs

Future Active Indicative

To conjugate the future active indicative verb, the primary active endings are suffixed to the tense stem which is found by dropping the "ω" from the second principal part. The following is the conjugation of the future active indicative of λύω:

	Singular	Plural
1.	λύσω	λύσομεν
2.	λύσεις	λύσετε
3.	λύσει	λύσουσι (ν)

Aorist Active Indicative

First Aorist

The third principal part is the aorist active indicative, and it may be either a first or second aorist. It is a secondary tense; hence, it uses the augment and secondary personal endings. The first aorist is formed by suffixing σα to the verb stem. Thus, the first aorist active indicative of λύω is ἔλυσα, and it is conjugated:

	Singular	Plural
1.	ἔλυσα	ἐλύσαμεν
2.	ἔλυσας	ἐλύσατε
3.	ἔλυσε (ν)	ἔλυσαν

Observe:
    1. The first person singular does not use the secondary active ending "ν."
    2. Instead of an "α," an "ε" stands in the third singular.

When the stem of a verb ends with a consonant, the addition of the σα suffix generally causes the following changes (the addition of the "ς" for the future tense stem causes the same changes):

25

1. If a verb stem ends with a labial mute* (π, β, φ), the final letter becomes a "ψ;" for example, γράφω becomes γράψω for the future and ἔγραψα for the first aorist.
2. If a verb stem ends with a palatal mute (κ, γ, χ), it becomes a "ξ:" ἄρχω becomes ἄρξω and ἦρξα.
3. If the verb stem ends with a dental mute (τ, δ, θ), it is dropped: πείθω becomes πείσω and ἔπεισα.
4. If a verb stem ends with a sibilant, those consonants having an "s" sound (ς, ζ, ξ, ψ), it is dropped: σώζω becomes σώσω and ἔσωσα.

<u>Second Aorist</u>

The second aorist stem is usually a shortened primitive stem: βάλλω has the aorist stem βαλ. The second aorist differs from the first in form only and not in meaning; hence, only a few verbs have both a first and second aorist. It cannot be predetermined by examining the vocabulary form whether a verb has a first or seond aorist stem; this is a matter of vocabulary study. The second aorist active indicative conjugation of βάλλω is:

	Singular	Plural
1.	ἔβαλον	ἐβάλομεν
2.	ἔβαλες	ἐβάλετε
3.	ἔβαλε (ν)	ἔβαλον

Observe:
1. This conjugation uses the augment and variable vowels.
2. Except for the different tense stem, the conjugations of the second aorist and the imperfect are identical.

Principal Parts

It is difficult to overstress the importance of learning the principal parts of a verb. Although there are certain tendencies that are usually followed, such as with the mute stems, it is impossible to predict with certainty the form of a principal part. However, the Greek language is not alone; the principal parts of an English verb are formed in various unpredictable ways.

---

* A mute is a consonant that indicates a complete stop of the sound. A labial mute is formed with the lips; a palatal with the palate; a dental with the teeth.

Even though the principal parts of a verb may be irregular, once the tense stem is known, the verb is conjugated like λύω. Compare the conjugations of the future active indicatives of εὑρίσκω and λύω.

	Singular		Plural	
1.	εὑρήσω	λύσω	εὑρήσομεν	λύσομεν
2.	εὑρήσεις	λύσεις	εὑρήσετε	λύσετε
3.	εὑρήσει	λύσει	εὑρήσουσι (ν)	λύσουσι (ν)

Translation of the Tenses

The future tense signifies that an action (usually undefined) will occur in future time.

The first and second aorist indicate that an undefined action* has occured in past time. This tense may be expressed by the English perfect, pluperfect, or the past tense. The Greek context will usually indicate which English tense should be used in translation.

These sentences from Mark and Plato illustrate the difference between the aorist and the imperfect.

ὅτε **ἔδυ** ὁ ἥλιος, **ἔφερον** πρὸς αὐτὸ πάντας τοὺς κακῶς ἔχοντας (Mark 1:32); "When the sun **had set**, they **were bringing** to him all the sick."

When Mark used the second aorist ἔδυ, he did not place stress on a particular kind of action; he simply presented the fact that in past time the sun set. However, when he wanted to describe the people who were going through the process of bringing their sick to Jesus, he used the imperfect ἔφερον: in past time a steady stream of the sick were being brought to him.

Plato has Socrates stating:

ὀλίγου ἐμαυτοῦ **ἐπελαθόμην** · οὕτω πιθανῶς **ἔλεγον** (The Apology I:3-5);

"I almost **forgot** myself; so persuasively **were** they **speaking**."

Socrates said that in past time he nearly forgot himself (second aorist middle verb ἐπελαθόμην). The reason for this is that in the past his accusers were going through a process of persuasive speaking (imperfect active verb ἔλεγον).

---

* The term "aorist" (from ἀ + ὁριστός) means "undefined" which indicates that the action is stated without describing it. The aorist and imperfect tenses may be compared with cameras to illustrate their different kinds of action. The aorist presents the action somewhat like a snap shot; the imperfect gives a moving picture.

Vocabulary

1. ἄγγελος, ου, ὁ — messenger or angel (angel)
2. ἀλλά, conjuction — but
3. βασιλεία, ας, ἡ — kingdom (basilica)
4. γῆ, ῆς, ἡ — earth or land (geology)
5. ἔργον, ου, τό — work (energy)
6. βάλλω, --, ἔβαλον, throw, (ballistic)
7. γράφω, γράψω, ἔγραψα, write, (γραφή)
8. εἶδον, second aorist active of the obsolete verb εἴδω, see
9. εἶπον, second aorist active of the obsolete verb ἔπω, say (epic)
10. ἔλαβον, second aorist active of λαμβάνω, take or receive
11. ἐσθίω, --, ἔφαγον, eat, (anthropophagous)
12. εὑρίσκω, εὑρήσω, εὗρον, find, (eureka)
13. ἔχω [the imperfect is εἶχον], ἕξω or σχήσω, ἔσχον, have, (scheme)
14. λέγω, λέξω, ἔλεξα, say or speak, (lexicon)
15. σώζω, σώσω, ἔσωσα, save, (sozin)

Translation

1. The good women were receiving the kingdom of God, but the other women did not receive the kingdom.
2. We shall write the words of authority to the master of the kingdom, but you wrote to the apostles' church.
3. Sir, the holy men were having works of love, and I did not have love, but you will have good works for the holy god.
4. The good angels of heaven saved the first man of the land for the Lord, and we shall not save the other messenger's brother, but the holy writing is not saving the men of sin.
5. εὗρον τὴν καλὴν γῆν οἱ υἱοὶ τῆς ἄλλης βασιλείας ἀλλὰ οὐχ εὑρήσουσιν οἱ μαθηταὶ ἁμαρτίας τὸ δῶρον καλῆς εἰρήνης.

6. τούς πρώτους λόγους τοῦ νόμου ἔλεξα τῷ καλῷ καὶ λέγετε τοὺς λόγους ἔργων ἀλλὰ αἱ πρῶται ἐκκλησίαι λέξουσι τοὺς λόγους ἀγάπης καὶ ἀληθείας τοῖς ἀγαθοῖς ἀδελφοῖς τῆς νεκρᾶς.
7. ἤσθιον τὰ ἀγαθὰ τῆς καλῆς ἐρήμου ἀλλὰ ἔφαγες τὰ νεκρὰ τῆς γῆς.
8. ἐπιστεύομεν τῇ ἐξουσίᾳ τῶν ἁγίων τῶν ἀγγέλων τοῦ οὐρανοῦ.
9. ὁ ἅγιος καὶ ἀγαθὸς θεὸς τὰ ὅλα ἔργα τοῦ καλοῦ προφήτου εἶδεν;
10. οἱ ἄγγελοι εἶπον Ἔργα οὐ σώσουσιν τοὺς προφήτας τῆς ἁμαρτίας τῷ θεῷ ἀλλὰ ἔσωσε τοὺς ὄχλους ἡ ἀγάπη τοῦ ἁγίου τοῦ θεοῦ.
11. τὸ δῶρον οἱ ἄλλοι μαθηταὶ τοῦ προφήτου ἔβαλλον καὶ ἐβάλετε τὸ δῶρον ἀλλὰ οὐ βάλλω ἄλλα δῶρα.
12. εἶδες τὰ ἔργα τοῦ ὄχλου καὶ τοὺς λόγους τῆς πρώτης βασιλείας τοῖς ἀποστόλοις τοῦ κυρίου ἔγραφες.
13. τοὺς λόγους τῆς ψυχῆς ἔσχετε καὶ εἶχον τοὺς λόγους ἀλλὰ οἱ ἄνθρωποι τῆς γῆς οὐχ ἕξουσιν.
14. ὁ πρῶτος προφήτης καὶ ὁ ἀγαθὸς νεανίας τὰς ὥρας ἡμέρας σώσει.
15. τὴν βασιλείαν τοῦ θεοῦ ἐδόξασεν (δοξάζω, glorify) ὁ ἀγαθὸς στρατιώτης (στρατιώτης, ου, ὁ, soldier).
16. τῇ γλώσσῃ (γλῶσσα, ης, ἡ, tongue) οἱ υἱοὶ ἁμαρτίας τοὺς υἱοὺς ἀληθείας διώξουσιν (διώκω, persecute).
17. ἐπιστρέψομεν (ἐπιστρέφω, turn) ἰσχυροὺς (ἰσχυρός, ά, όν, strong) ἀνθρώπους τῷ θεῷ τοῦ οὐρανοῦ.
18. αἱ ἰσχυραὶ τοὺς λῃστὰς (λῃστής, οῦ, ὁ, robber) τῷ νόμῳ ἐπιστρέψουσιν.

John 4:2

Ἰησοῦς (Jesus, Nom. s.) αὐτὸς (himself) οὐκ ἐβάπτιζεν (βαπτίζω, baptize) ἀλλ' (but) οἱ μαθηταὶ αὐτοῦ (his). KJV: "Jesus himself baptized not, but his disciples."

Luke 4:2

καὶ οὐκ ἔφαγεν οὐδέν (anything, acc.).

Luke 6:1

ἔτιλλον (τίλλω, pick) οἱ μαθηταὶ αὐτοῦ (his) καὶ ἤσθιον τοὺς στάχυας (heads of grain, acc.).

Chapter VII

Perfect and Pluperfect Active Indicative

Dative of Means

The objects of ἀκούω and πιστεύω

Perfect Active Indicative
The perfect and pluperfect are formed on the fourth of the principal parts. The perfect active indicative conjugation of λύω is:

	Singular	Plural
1.	λέλυκα	λελύκαμεν
2.	λέλυκας	λελύκατε
3.	λέλυκε (ν)	λέλυκαν or λελύκασι (ν)

Reduplication
A noticeable characteristic of the perfect tense is reduplication. The majority of the verbs whose present tense stem begins with a consonant are reduplicated by prefixing the beginning consonant and an "ε" to the stem: the perfect active indicative of λύω is λέλυκα, and γράφω is γέγραφα.

Verbs beginning with an aspirate (θ, φ, or χ) prefix the unaspirated form of the consonant and an "ε," that is, the perfect active of θαυμάζω is τεθαύμακα; φανερόω is πεφανέρωκα; χαίρω is κεχάρηκα.*

Verbs beginning with a double consonant (ζ, ξ, or ψ) and a few verbs beginning with two consonants reduplicate by prefixing an "ε:" the perfect active of ζητέω is ἐζήτηκα; στέλλω is ἔσταλκα.

Verbs that begin with a vowel reduplicate by lengthening the beginning vowel: the perfect of ἀγαπάω is ἠγάπηκα; ἐρωτάω is ἠρώτηκα; and ὁμολογέω is ὡμολόγηκα.

---

* This form appears only in Epic Greek; however, it does illustrate this rule of reduplication.

The κα suffix

The κα suffix is another identifying characteristic of the fourth principal part. The addition of the κα to the stem, particularly a stem ending with a consonant, may cause certain changes; for example, the "ζ" of σώζω drops when the κα is suffixed: σέσωκα. Although the changes that occur may be predicted with some degree of accuracy, it is necessary to make the fourth principal part a matter of vocabulary study.

A few perfect verbs, such as γέγραφα and οἶδα, do not have the "κ" in their tense stem. These are called second perfects, and the absence of the "κ" is also a matter of vocabulary study. The indicative conjugations of the perfect active of σώζω and the second perfect active of οἶδα are:

	Singular	Plural
1.	σέσωκα	σεσώκαμεν
2.	σέσωκας	σεσώκατε
3.	σέσωκε (ν)	σέσωκαν or σεσώκασι (ν)

	Singular	Plural
1.	οἶδα	οἴδαμεν
2.	οἶδας	οἴδατε
3.	οἶδε (ν)	οἶδαν or οἴδασι (ν)

Note that, except for the variations in the tense stems of οἶδα and σώζω, the perfect active indicative conjugations of λύω, οἶδα, and σώζω are the same.

Pluperfect Active Indicative

The pluperfect active indicative conjugation of λύω is:

	Singular	Plural
1.	(ἐ)λελύκειν	(ἐ)λελύκειμεν
2.	(ἐ)λελύκεις	(ἐ)λελύκειτε
3.	(ἐ)λελύκει	(ἐ)λελύκεισαν

Observe:
1. The pluperfect is sometimes formed without an augment.*
2. The suffix is κει.

---

* The Pluperfect occurs with 22 verbs in the New Testament and 15 have the augment.

Translation of the Tenses

The perfect tense in the indicative signifies that an action has been completed, and the results of this action remain until the present time. Therefore, the Greek perfect differs from the English perfect, which signifies completed action. The student of Greek should carefully note this distinction. In the English sentence "I have liberated the man," the subject has liberated the object, but the results of the liberating do not necessarily remain. In the Greek sentence λέλυκα τὸν ἄνθρωπον, the results of the subject's liberating the object remain up to the time of the statement; very likely "the man" is still liberated. However, the context indicates what the results are that remain, and each translation must be made in light of its context. The following sentences illustrate translations of the Greek perfect:

ὅ τι... **πεπόνθατε** ὑπὸ τῶν ἐμῶν κατηγόρων, οὐκ **οἶδα** (The Apology I: 1,2); "How... you **have been affected** by my accusers, I do not **know**."

ἤγγικεν ἡ βασιλεία τοῦ θεοῦ (Mark 1:15); "The kingdom of God **is near**."

The pluperfect is the past of the perfect tense. It points out that an action was completed, and the results from this action remained until some point in past time. The pluperfect is relatively rare; but when it occurs, translate it as the English pluperfect or the simple past tense.

Dative of Means

The dative case without a preposition may express means. This construction is usually impersonal.

καὶ ἐθεράπευσεν πολλοὺς κακῶς ἔχοντας ποικίλαις **νόσοις** (Mark 1:34); "And he healed many who were sick **by means of** various **diseases**."

ἐξελεγχθήσονται **ἔργῳ** (The Apology I:10); "They will be refuted **by** (by means of) a **deed**."

Objects of πιστεύω and ἀκούω

The object of πιστεύω is in the dative case.

διὰ τί οὖν οὐκ **ἐπιστεύσατε αὐτῷ**; (Mark 11:31); "Why, therefore, did you not **believe him**?"

The object of ἀκούω may be in either the genitive or accusative case.

ἀκούσεσθε πᾶσαν τὴν **ἀλήθειαν** (The Apology I:17); "You will **hear** all the **truth**."

ἀκούετε αὐτοῦ (Mark 9:7); "**Hear him**."

There are other verbs that have their objects in the genitive or dative cases. There are grammatical reasons for this, but it will suffice for now to learn these verbs and the case they require as they occur in the vocabulary.

Vocabulary

1. ἄρτος, ου, ὁ   bread
2. δικαιοσύνη, ης, ἡ   righteousness
3. δοῦλος, ου, ὁ   slave   (hierodule)
4. ἕτερος, α, ον   other   (heterodoxy)
5. θάλασσα, ης, ἡ   sea or lake   (thalassic)
6. καρδία, ας, ἡ   heart   (cardiac)
7. ἄγω, ἄξω, ἤγαγον, ἦχα, lead, (demagogue)
8. ἀκήκοα, perfect active indicative of ἀκούω, hear
9. βαπτίζω, βαπτίσω, ἐβάπτισα, βεβάπτικα, baptize, (baptize)
10. γέγραφα, second perfect active indicative of γράφω, write
11. ἑόρακα or ἑώρακα, perfect active indicative of ὁράω, see
12. οἶδα [οἶδα like the aorist εἶδον is from εἴδω; however, the perfect refers to seeing with the mind] know
13. πέμπω, πέμψω, ἔπεμψα, πέπομφα, send, (pompous)
14. πίπτω, --, ἔπεσον, πέπτωκα, fall

Translation

1. You have written words of righteousness for the glory of the Lord, and we have sacrificed (θύω, sacrifice) for the Lord.
2. By works of love the good God of heaven has led the sons of men, and they believe God's words.
3. τοῖς καλοῖς δούλοις πεπόμφασιν οἱ ἄλλοι νεανίαι τὰ δῶρα εἰρήνης.
4. ἀκήκοαν καρδίαις ἀγάπης τὰς καλὰς παραβολὰς δικαιοσύνης οἱ ἀγαθοὶ ἀδελφοί.
5. ἀκούομεν τῆς φωνῆς τῆς θαλάσσης καὶ γεγράφαμεν τοὺς καλοὺς λόγους ταῖς καρδίαις τῶν δούλων.

6. τοὺς υἱοὺς τοῦ ἀγαθοῦ ἀδελφοῦ οἶδεν ὁ ἕτερος προφήτης καὶ βαπτίσει θαλάσσῃ τοὺς υἱοὺς τῷ ἁγίῳ τῷ θεῷ.

7. ἐβεβαπτίκεις τὰς ἄλλας τῷ κυρίῳ ἀλλὰ οὐχ ἑώρακας τὰς ἑτέρας τῆς ἁμαρτίας.

8. ἄξω τοὺς ἀγαθοὺς καὶ ἤγαγες τοὺς ἄλλους ἀλλὰ οἱ δοῦλοι δικαιοσύνης ἤχασιν τὰς ἁγίας.

9. εἶπες, Ἀκούομεν τὴν καρδίαν τοῦ ἀνθρώπου τῆς θαλάσσης ἀλλὰ οὐκ ἐσθίει ἄρτον.

10. τοὺς ἀγαθοὺς δούλους βεβαπτίκασιν οἱ ἀπόστολοι τοῦ κυρίου, βαπτίσω τοὺς ἑτέρους δούλους, καὶ βαπτίζεις τοὺς ἄλλους.

11. φωνῇ ἀγάπης σεσώκαμεν τὰ ἅγια ἱερὰ τοῖς ἀποστόλοις τοῖς ἀγαθοῖς εἰρήνης.

12. οὐ πεπίστευκαν τοῖς λόγοις τῆς ἡμέρας οἱ ὄχλοι τῆς βασιλείας.

13. πεπαίδευκαν (παιδεύω, educate) τὰ παιδία (παιδίον, ου, τό, child) οἱ σοφοὶ (σοφός, ή, όν, wise) τοῖς λόγοις ἀληθείας.

14. τὰ σοφὰ παιδία τὴν δικαιοσύνην θεοῦ ἠγάπηκεν (ἀγαπάω, love).

15. τὸν ἀγαθὸν ἄρτον πεφιλήκασιν (φιλέω, love) οἱ σοφοὶ υἱοὶ τῆς καλῆς βασιλείας καὶ οἱ ἀπόστολοι τῶν υἱῶν.

16. πεποίθαμεν (πείθω, persuade) τὰ παιδία καὶ τὸν κύριον ἐφίλησαν.

I Cor. 15:3-4

παρέδωκα (I delivered) γὰρ (for) ὑμῖν (to you) . . . ὅτι (that) Χριστὸς (Χριστός, οῦ, ὁ, Christ) ἀπέθανεν (2nd aor. act. ind. 3 s., die) . . . καὶ ὅτι ἐγήγερται (perf. pass. ind. 3 s., raise).

John 19:22

ἀπεκρίθη (answered) ὁ Πιλᾶτος (Πιλᾶτος, ου, ὁ, Pilate), ῝Ο (what) γέγραφα, γέγραφα.

John 20:29

Ὅτι (because) ἑώρακάς με (me) πεπίστευκας;

Rev. 2:5

μνημόνευε (remember) οὖν (therefore) πόθεν (from where) πέπτωκας.

Chapter VIII

Passive Voice
Genitive of Personal Agent
Postpositives
Historical Present

Passive Voice

The personal endings for the passive voice are:

	Primary		Secondary	
	Singular	Plural	Singular	Plural
1.	μαι	μεθα	μην	μεθα
2.	σαι	σθε	σο	σθε
3.	ται	νται	το	ντο

Early in the history of the Greek language, there was a tendency to drop the "σ" in the second person singular of both the primary and the secondary endings. Therefore, special attention should be given to the second person singulars in the following conjugations of the indicative mood:

	Present Passive		Imperfect Passive	
	Singular	Plural	Singular	Plural
1.	λύομαι	λυόμεθα	ἐλυόμην	ἐλυόμεθα
2.	λύῃ (ει)	λύεσθε	ἐλύου	ἐλύεσθε
3.	λύεται	λύονται	ἐλύετο	ἐλύοντο

Observe:
1. The present and imperfect passives are built upon the first of the principal parts.
2. Augments and variable vowels appear in the appropriate places.

	Perfect Passive		Pluperfect Passive	
	Singular	Plural	Singular	Plural
1.	λέλυμαι	λελύμεθα	(ἐ)λελύμην	(ἐ)λελύμεθα
2.	λέλυσαι	λέλυσθε	(ἐ)λέλυσο	(ἐ)λέλυσθε
3.	λέλυται	λέλυνται	(ἐ)λέλυτο	(ἐ)λέλυντο

Observe:
1. The perfect and pluperfect passives are formed on the fifth principal part.
2. The fifth principal part, like the fourth, has reduplication; however, it does not have the κα.
3. The personal endings are added directly to the tense stem without variable vowels.

	First Aorist Passive		Future Passive	
	Singular	Plural	Singular	Plural
1.	ἐλύθην	ἐλύθημεν	λυθήσομαι	λυθησόμεθα
2.	ἐλύθης	ἐλύθητε	λυθήσῃ (ει)	λυθήσεσθε
3.	ἐλύθη	ἐλύθησαν	λυθήσεται	λυθήσονται

Observe:
1. The aorist passive and the future passive are formed on the sixth of the principal parts.
2. The aorist passive has the augment but uses secondary active endings.
3. The future passive stem is formed by adding "σ" to the unaugmented form.
4. The future passive uses variable vowels and primary passive endings.

	Second Aorist Passive		Second Future Passive	
	Singular	Plural	Singular	Plural
1.	ἐγράφην	ἐγράφημεν	γραφήσομαι	γραφησόμεθα
2.	ἐγράφης	ἐγράφητε	γραφήσῃ (ει)	γραφήσεσθε
3.	ἐγράφη	ἐγράφησαν	γραφήσεται	γραφήσονται

Observe:
1. The sixth principal part of a few verbs has η and not θη as a suffix; except for the missing "θ," the aorist and future passive conjugations of these verbs are the same as the aorist and future passive conjugations of other "ω" verbs.
2. A second aorist verb in the third principal part will not necessarily be second aorist in the sixth principal part.

The passive voice signifies that the subject receives the action. The significance of tense is the same for the passive voice as for the active voice.

λύομαι	(present)	"I am liberated" or "I am being liberated."
ἐλυόμην	(imperfect)	"I was being liberated."
λέλυμαι	(perfect)	"I have been liberated" or "I am liberated."
ἐλελύμην	(pluperfect)	"I had been liberated" or "I was liberated."
ἐλύθην	(aorist)	"I was liberated."
λυθήσομαι	(future)	"I shall be liberated."

Genitive of Personal Agent

Personal agent for the passive voice is expressed by the preposition ὑπό with the genitive.

> Ἰησοῦς ... ἐβαπτίσθη ... ὑπὸ Ἰωάννου (Mark 1:9); "Jesus ... was baptized ... **by John.**"

When the agent is impersonal, the dative of means is usually used. The distinction between the dative of means and the genitive of personal agent is seen in the following statement:

> ὑπ'ἐμοῦ ἐξελεγχθήσονται ἔργῳ (The Apology I:10); "**By me** they will be refuted **by means of a deed.**"

Postpositives

A word that cannot stand first in its clause is called a postpositive.

> χωρὶς δὲ παραβολῆς οὐκ ἐλάλει αὐτοῖς, κατ' ἰδίαν δὲ τοῖς ἰδίοις μαθηταῖς ἐπέλυεν πάντα (Mark 4:34); "**But** apart from a parable he was not speaking to them, **but** privately to his own disciples he was explaining all things."

If a word is postpositive, it will be designated as such in the vocabulary.

Historical Present

For the sake of vividness, quite often in Greek narrative the present tense in the indicative mood is used for a past event. An English translator normally uses a past tense when translating the Greek historical present.

> ἡ δὲ πενθερὰ Σίμωνος κατέκειτο πυρέσσουσα, καὶ εὐθὺς **λέγουσιν** αὐτῷ περὶ αὐτῆς (Mark 1:30); "And because of being feverish, Simon's mother-in-law was lying down, and immediately they **told** him about her."

Vocabulary

1. ἀγαπητός, ή, όν — beloved
2. δέ, postpositive conjunction — and or but
3. δίκαιος, α, ον — just or righteous
4. ἔτι, adverb — still or yet
5. ἕτοιμος, η, ον — prepared or ready
6. εὐαγγέλιον, ου, τό — gospel (evangelist)
7. ἤ, conjunction — or
8. καιρός, οῦ, ὁ — season or time
9. κεφαλή, ῆς, ἡ — head (cephalic)
10. κόσμος, ου, ὁ — world (cosmic)
11. λαός, οῦ, ὁ — people (laity)
12. ὀφθαλμός, οῦ, ὁ — eye (ophthalmology)
13. πονηρός, ά, όν — evil
14. πρόσωπον, ου, τό — face (prosopography)
15. σημεῖον, ου, τό — sign (semaphore)
16. τέκνον, ου, τό — child (teknonymy)
17. τόπος, ου, ὁ — place (topic)
18. ὑπό, preposition followed by the genitive case — by

Translation

1. The beloved woman is led by the righteous man, but I have led the people by the signs of the world.
2. Was the gospel being believed by the people of the evil place?
3. I still believe the gospel of truth, and it will lead men to the prepared place.
4. ὁ καιρὸς ἡμέρας οὐ γινώσκεται ὑπὸ τῶν τέκνων τοῦ μαθητοῦ, τὰ δὲ τέκνα οἶδαν τὴν δόξαν τῆς ἁγίας ὥρας.
5. ἔτι οἱ οἶκοι τῶν ἁγίων λύονται ὑπὸ τοῦ πονηροῦ υἱοῦ ἢ τοῦ ἑτέρου τέκνου.
6. ἐβαπτιζόμεθα ὑπ' ἀγαθοῦ προφήτου καὶ ἐλαμβάνομεν τὸ εὐαγγέλιον ταῖς καρδίαις ἀγάπης.

7. οἱ λόγοι δικαιοσύνης ἐπεπίστευντο καὶ βλέψομεν τὸν κύριον τοῦ οὐρανοῦ καὶ τῆς γῆς.

8. ἐσώθησαν οἱ ἀγαπητοὶ μαθηταὶ ὑπὸ τοῦ νεκροῦ τοῦ δούλου· ὁ δὲ δίκαιος ἀδελφὸς σωθήσεται τοῖς σημείοις τοῦ θεοῦ.

9. βεβαπτίσμεθα ὑπὸ τοῦ πονηροῦ υἱοῦ ἀλλὰ σεσώσμεθα ὑπὸ τοῦ ἀγαθοῦ κυρίου.

10. τοῖς ὀφθαλμοῖς ἑόρακε τὸ πρόσωπον καὶ τὴν κεφαλὴν τῆς καλῆς ὁ νεανίας.

11. οὐκ ἐλέλυντο οἱ δίκαιοι δοῦλοι ὑπὸ τοῦ πονηροῦ ἀγγέλου τῆς ἐκκλησίας.

12. τὸ εὐαγγέλιον τοῦ κυρίου τῇ ἐξουσίᾳ τῆς ἀγαπητῆς κεφαλῆς τῆς ἐκκλησίας ἐγράφη τῷ ἁγίῳ τῷ θεῷ.

13. ἐδιδάχθη ὑπὸ τοῦ πρώτου λαοῦ τοῦ κόσμου τῇ βασιλείᾳ τοῦ θεοῦ τὰ τέκνα, ἀκηκόαμεν δὲ τῶν καλῶν λόγων δικαιοσύνης.

14. τότε (then) ἐφυλάχθησαν (φυλάσσω, guard) τοῖς δικαίοις νόμοις τῆς καλῆς τῆς βασιλείας οἱ ὀφθαλμοὶ τοῦ ἀγαπητοῦ λαοῦ.

15. ὁ πονηρὸς νόμος τῆς γῆς πέπρακται (πράσσω, practice) ὑπὸ τοῦ ἑτέρου λαοῦ ἀλλὰ ἄλλον νόμον ἔτι πράσσομεν.

16. ἑτοιμασθήσονται (ἑτμοιμάζω, prepare) οἱ οὐρανοὶ καὶ ὁ κόσμος ὑπὸ τοῦ ἁγίου τέκνου.

Matt 11:19

καὶ ἐδικαιώθη (δικαιόω, justify) ἡ σοφία (σοφία, ας, ἡ, wisdom) . . . τῶν ἔργων αὐτῆς (her).

Rom. 2:13

οἱ ποιηταὶ (ποιητής, οῦ, ὁ, doer) νόμου δικαιωθήσονται (δικαιόω, justify).

Rom 3:21

δικαιοσύνη θεοῦ πεφανέρωται (φανερόω, show) . . . ὑπὸ τοῦ νόμου καὶ τῶν προφητῶν.

I Cor. 11:32

ὑπὸ τοῦ κυρίου παιδευόμεθα (παιδεύω, teach).

Chapter IX

Middle Voice
Deponent Verbs
Context

Middle Voice

The personal endings for the middle voice are the same as those for the passive voice.

	Primary		Secondary	
	Singular	Plural	Singular	Plural
1.	μαι	μεθα	μην	μεθα
2.	σαι	σθε	σο	σθε
3.	ται	νται	το	ντο

Observe that it is necessary again to give special attention to the second person singular.

The present and imperfect middles are formed on the first of the principal parts.

	Present Middle		Imperfect Middle	
	Singular	Plural	Singular	Plural
1.	λύομαι	λυόμεθα	ἐλυόμην	ἐλυόμεθα
2.	λύῃ (ει)	λύεσθε	ἐλύου	ἐλύεσθε
3.	λύεται	λύονται	ἐλύετο	ἐλύοντο

The future middle is formed on the second of the principal parts.

	Singular	Plural
1.	λύσομαι	λυσόμεθα
2.	λύσῃ (ει)	λύσεσθε
3.	λύσεται	λύσονται

The aorist middle is formed on the third of the principal parts.

	First Aorist Middle		Second Aorist Middle	
	Singular	Plural	Singular	Plural
1.	ἐλυσάμην	ἐλυσάμεθα	ἐβαλόμην	ἐβαλόμεθα
2.	ἐλύσω	ἐλύσασθε	ἐβάλου	ἐβάλεσθε
3.	ἐλύσατο	ἐλύσαντο	ἐβάλετο	ἐβάλοντο

The perfect and pluperfect middles are formed on the fifth of the principal parts.

	Perfect Middle		Pluperfect Middle	
	Singular	Plural	Singular	Plural
1.	λέλυμαι	λελύμεθα	(ἐ)λελύμην	(ἐ)λελύμεθα
2.	λέλυσαι	λέλυσθε	(ἐ)λέλυσο	(ἐ)λέλυσθε
3.	λέλυται	λέλυνται	(ἐ)λέλυτο	(ἐ)λέλυντο

The middle voice signifies that the subject does the action with special interest to itself. The particular verb and context indicate what this special interest is. Sometimes the difference between the active and the middle is too minute for translation into English. Usually though, the subject does something for itself, to itself, or to something belonging to itself. Since English does not have the middle voice, there is not one translation that may be given that will suffice every time the middle occurs. The following sentences illustrate some of the possible translations.

    ἀπήγξατο (Matthew 27:5); "**He hanged himself.**"

This sentence is from the passage that tells of Judas' suicide. The context and the meaning of the verb clearly indicate that Judas did the action to himself. Compare:

    ἐκαλλυνόμην τε καὶ **ἠβρυνόμην** (The Apology IV:32); "I **was** both **pluming** and **priding** myself."

    καὶ **περιεβλέπετο** ἰδεῖν τὴν τοῦτο ποιήσασαν (Mark 5:32); "And he **was looking around** to see the woman who had done this."

In this sentence the middle voice is used because the subject does the action for himself. The active voice is adequate for the English translation. Compare:

    μάρτυρας . . .ὑμῶν τοὺς πολλοὺς **παρέχομαι** (The Apology III:19,20); "**I present** the many of you . . . as witnesses."

    ἀλλ᾽ οὐδενὸς λόγου **ποιοῦμαι** τὴν ψυχὴν (Acts 20:24); "But **I make** my life of no account."

The writer of this sentence uses the middle voice because the subject acts upon his own life. Compare:

οὐ γὰρ νίπτονται τὰς χεῖρας αὐτῶν (Matthew 15:2); "For they **are** not **washing** their hands."

Deponent Verbs

Certain verbs are given in the vocabulary with a middle or passive form where an active form is anticipated; that is, for the verb "come" the first of the principal parts is ἔρχομαι and not ἔρχω. Such verbs are called deponents. These verbs are middle or passive in form but active in meaning. Study the following verbs:

ἀσπάζομαι, ἀσπάσομαι, ἠσπασάμην, --, --, --, salute
ἔρχομαι, ἐλεύσομαι, ἦλθον, ἐλήλυθα, --, --, come or go
πίνω, πίομαι, ἔπιον, πέπωκα, πέπομαι, ἐπόθην, drink

ἀσπάζομαι is deponent in the first three principal parts. ἔρχομαι is deponent in the first two, and πίνω is deponent only in the second principal part.

The sixth principal part of a few verbs is deponent: ἀπεκρίθην "answer."

καλῶς **ἀπεκρίθη** αὐτοῖς (Mark 12:28); "He **answered** them well."

Context

In Greek, as in English, the context is very important.* It may be the primary factor in determining whether a verb has passive or middle voice. Normally the context indicates what the results are that remain when the perfect tense is used. A large number of Greek words have multiple vocabulary meanings, and the context aids in choosing the proper translation. It also may help the cases express their various uses; that is, it indicates whether a dative noun will be the dative of means or the indirect object. In the early development of the language the context was used to indicate the time of action. Only when the context failed to point out past time was the augment used. As new areas of study are introduced, the importance of the context will be seen again and again.

---

* The linquist Mario Pei maintains that in normal conversation the hearer really hears only about 50 percent of what the speaker says and supplies the rest out of his own sense of the context. *The Sound of Language,* p. 107.

Vocabulary

The following list contains no new vocabulary words but completes the principal parts of the verbs that have been given in the preceding chapters. The forms which have an asterisk have peculiarities that have not been discussed.

1. ἄγω, ἄξω, ἤγαγον, ἦχα, ἦγμαι, ἤχθην, lead
2. ἀκούω, ἀκούσω, ἤκουσα, ἀκήκοα, --, ἠκούσθην, hear
3. βάλλω, βαλῶ*, ἔβαλον, βέβληκα, βέβλημαι, ἐβλήθην, throw
4. βαπτίζω, βαπτίσω, ἐβάπτισα, βεβάπτικα, βεβάπτισμαι, ἐβαπτίσθην, baptize
5. βλέπω, βλέψω, ἔβλεψα, --, --, --, see
6. γιγνώσκω or γινώσκω, γνώσομαι, ἔγνων*, ἔγνωκα, ἔγνωσμαι, ἐγνώσθην, know
7. γράφω, γράψω, ἔγραψα, γέγραφα, γέγραμμαι, ἐγράφην, write
8. διδάσκω, διδάξω, ἐδίδαξα, δεδίδαχα, δεδίδαγμαι, ἐδιδάχθην, teach
9. ἐσθίω, φάγομαι, ἔφαγον, --, --, --, eat
10. εὑρίσκω, εὑρήσω, εὗρον, εὕρηκα, εὕρημαι, εὑρέθην, find
11. ἔχω [the imperfect is εἶχον], ἕξω or σχήσω, ἔσχον, ἔσχηκα, --, --, have
12. λαμβάνω, λήμψομαι, ἔλαβον, εἴληφα, εἴλημμαι, ἐλήμφθην, take or receive
13. λέγω, λέξω, ἔλεξα, --, λέλεγμαι, ἐλέχθην, say
14. λύω, λύσω, ἔλυσα, λέλυκα, λέλυμαι, ἐλύθην, destroy or liberate
15. πέμπω, πέμψω, ἔπεμψα, πέπομφα, πέπεμμαι, ἐπέμφθην, send
16. πίπτω, πεσοῦμαι*, ἔπεσον, πέπτωκα, --, --, fall
17. πιστεύω, πιστεύσω, ἐπίστευσα, πεπίστευκα, πεπίστευμαι, ἐπιστεύθην, believe or trust
18. σώζω, σώσω, ἔσωσα, σέσωκα, σέσωσμαι, ἐσώθην, save

Translation

1. The evil children will know the beloved gospel and will be saved by the Lord.
2. The just slave taught himself the law of the land.
3. Shall we still receive the bread of life?

4. δεδίδαγται τὰ σημεῖα τοῦ θεοῦ ὑπὸ ἀγαπητοῦ μαθητοῦ τῷ λαῷ τοῦ κοσμοῦ.

5. δεδίδαγται τοὺς δικαίους νόμους τῆς ἐκκλησίας τῷ ὄχλῳ ἑτοίμων τέκνων ὁ ἄγγελος τοῦ κυρίου.

6. τὰ δὲ πονηρὰ τέκνα τοῦ ἀγαθοῦ προφήτου λημψόμεθα καρδίαις ἀγάπης ἀλλὰ οὐκ ἐλαμβάνεσθε τὰ τέκνα.

7. οἱ πονηροὶ δοῦλοι ἐλαμβάνοντο ἄρτον καὶ δῶρα, οἱ δὲ ἀγαθοὶ ἀπόστολοι σῴζονται τὸν λόγον τῆς ἀληθείας τῷ κυρίῳ.

8. ἡ ἑτοίμη εὑρήσεται ἀλλὰ εὑρέθητε ὑπὸ τοῦ πρώτου ἀποστόλου τοῦ κυρίου.

9. τὰ τέκνα ἐβαπτίσατο ὁ ἀγαθὸς υἱὸς τῇ βασιλείᾳ τοῦ κυρίου.

10. ὁ δὲ δίκαιος ἦγται ὑπὸ τοῦ μαθητοῦ τῇ δόξῃ οὐρανοῦ.

11. ἐλύσασθε τὴν κεφαλὴν τῆς ἐκκλησίας τοῖς λόγοις ἀληθείας;

12. ἠκουόμεθα τῶν φωνῶν τοῦ καιροῦ ἀλλὰ οὐκ ἠκούσθημεν ὑπὸ τοῦ λαοῦ τοῦ κόσμου.

13. τοὺς ἁγίους λόγους τῆς ζωῆς τοῖς ἀγαπητοῖς υἱοῖς ἐγραψάμην.

14. τοὺς μαθητὰς περὶ (prep. with gen., concerning) δικαιοσύνης ἀναμιμνήσκει (ἀναμιμνήσκω, remind) τὸ εὐαγγέλιον τοῦ κυρίου καὶ ἀναμιμνήσκομαι τοὺς ἀγαπητοὺς λόγους δικαιοσύνης.

15. ἔφαινον (φαίνω, show) οἱ δοῦλοι τὴν θάλασσαν τοῖς τέκνοις τότε (then) ἐφαίνοντο οἱ ἅγιοι ἄγγελοι τοῦ καλοῦ τοῦ οὐρανοῦ.

16. οἱ ἀδελφοὶ τοῦ πονηροῦ ἀνθρώπου κηρύσσειν (inf. to preach) ἔπεισαν (πείθω, persuade) τὸν νεανίαν καὶ οἱ ἄλλοι ἀδελφοὶ πείθονται τῷ ἀγαθῷ νεανίᾳ.

Mark 10:20

ἔφη (he said) αὐτῷ (to him), Διδάσκαλε, ταῦτα (these things) πάντα (all) ἐφυλαξάμην (φυλάσσω, keep).

James 4:3

αἰτεῖτε (αἰτέω, ask) καὶ οὐ λαμβάνετε, διότι (because) κακῶς (wrongly) αἰτεῖσθε (αἰτέω, ask).

Matt 15:2

οὐ γὰρ (for) νίπτονται (νίπτω, wash) τὰς χεῖρας (hands) αὐτῶν (their).

Romans 15:7

ὁ Χριστὸς (Χριστός, οῦ ὁ, Christ) προσελάβετο (προσλαμβάνω, 2nd aor. mid. ind. 3 s., accept) ὑμᾶς (you) εἰς (for) δόξαν τοῦ θεοῦ.

Chapter X

Personal Pronouns*
Declension of Ἰησοῦς
The Article Continued

Personal Pronouns

<u>Form</u>

A pronoun is a word that stands in place of a noun; when used properly, it eliminates the monotonous repetition of a noun. The personal pronouns are declined as follows:

	First Person	
	Singular	Plural
Nom.	ἐγώ	ἡμεῖς
Gen.	ἐμοῦ or μου	ἡμῶν
Dat.	ἐμοί or μοι	ἡμῖν
Acc.	ἐμέ or με	ἡμᾶς

	Second Person	
	Singular	Plural
Nom.	σύ	ὑμεῖς
Gen.	σοῦ or σου	ὑμῶν
Dat.	σοί or σοι	ὑμῖν
Acc.	σέ or σε	ὑμᾶς

Observe that the unaccented forms μου, μοι, με, and σου, σοι, σε should also be memorized.

---

* There are several distinct classes of pronouns: personal, relative, interrogative, etc. It will be beneficial to call these pronouns by their full name since the names usually explain the function of the various pronouns.

Third Person*

	Singular			Plural		
	Mas.	Fem.	Neuter	Mas.	Fem.	Neuter
Nom.	αὐτός	αὐτή	αὐτό	αὐτοί	αὐταί	αὐτά
Gen.	αὐτοῦ	αὐτῆς	αὐτοῦ	αὐτῶν	αὐτῶν	αὐτῶν
Dat.	αὐτῷ	αὐτῇ	αὐτῷ	αὐτοῖς	αὐταῖς	αὐτοῖς
Acc.	αὐτόν	αὐτήν	αὐτό	αὐτούς	αὐτάς	αὐτά

Enclitics

The genitive, dative, and accusative singulars of the first and second person personal pronouns have accented and unaccented forms. These unaccented forms are enclitics. An enclitic is a word that goes so closely with the word which it follows that it has no accent of its own. They require the following rules of accent:

1. An enclitic or proclitic before an enclitic has an acute on the ultima. καλόν **σέ ἐστιν** (Mark 9:47); ἐστιν is an enclitic; thus the enclitic σε is accented.
2. The word preceding an enclitic does not change an acute over the ultima to a grave: εἰ ὁ **υἱός μου** (Mark 1:11).
3. When the word preceding an enclitic has an acute over the antepenult or a circumflex over the penult, this word has an acute over the ultima: τὸν **ἄγγελόν μου**, πρὸ προσώπου σου (Mark 1:2); and **οἶδά σε** (Mark 1:24).

The accented forms of the first and second person personal pronouns are emphatic. Usually the emphatic form is used when emphasis or contrast is desired, and when the pronoun is used with a preposition.

Uses

Although English uses a personal pronoun as the subject of a sentence, when expressing the same idea in Greek, the inflection of the Greek verb adequately expresses the subject. A personal pronoun is seldom used in the

---

*Homeric Greek did not use αὐτός as a personal pronoun, but used a third person personal pronoun which was declined: singulars -- gen. οὗ, dat. οἷ, acc. ἑ; plurals -- nom. σφεῖς, gen. σφῶν, dat. σφίσι, acc. σφᾶς. Soon after the Homeric period, αὐτός began replacing the third person personal pronoun.

The oblique cases (genitive, dative, and accusative) of the personal pronouns may have the same functions that the corresponding cases of nouns have.

ἀποστέλλω τὸν ἄγγελόν **μου** πρὸ προσώπου **σου** (Mark 1:2); "I send **my** messenger before **your** face."

καὶ εἶπεν **αὐτοῖς** ὁ Ἰησοῦς (Mark 1:17); "And Jesus said **to them**."

οἶδά **σε** (Mark 1:24); "I know **you**."

A personal pronoun may intensify the subject pronoun expressed by the inflection of a verb.

ἐγὼ ἐβάπτισα ὑμᾶς (Mark 1:8); "**I myself** baptized you."

σὺ εἶ (second person singular of the verb "to be") ὁ υἱός μου (Mark 1:11); "**You yourself** are my son."

ἐπείνασεν **αὐτός** (Mark 2:25); "**He himself** hungered."

As can be noted in the three examples above, the intensifying pronouns agree with the person and number of their verbs. This is always true for ἐγώ and σύ; however, αὐτός may intensify the subject pronouns of the first and second person verbs.

αὐτὸς ἄρα νομίζω (The Apology XIV:14); "Then **I myself** believe."

ταῦτα γὰρ ἑωρᾶτε... **αὐτοί** (The Apology III:11); "For **you yourselves** were seeing... these things."

When the subject pronoun expressed in a verb is first or second person, it may be made doubly emphatic by using αὐτός with ἐγώ or σύ.

ἐγὼ δ'... **αὐτὸς**... ἐπελαθόμην (The Apology I:3,4); "But... **even I myself**... forgot."

δεῦτε **ὑμεῖς αὐτοί** (Mark 6:31); "Come, **even you yourselves**."

αὐτός may intensify a substantive in any case by modifying it in the predicate position.

αὐτὸς γὰρ ὁ **Ἡρῴδης**... ἐκράτησεν τὸν Ἰωάννην (Mark 6:17); "For **Herod himself** seized John."

φρονιμώτατος ἔσοιτο, μήτε τῶν τῆς πόλεως, πρὶν **αὐτῆς τῆς πόλεως** (gen. fem. sing. noun),... ἐπιμελεῖσθαι (The Apology XXVI:17-20); "It is best... to look after, not the things of the city, before the **city itself**."

αὐτός may modify a substantive in the attributive position, and it is translated "same."*

---

* In English the words *self* and *same* stand in the same position as they do in Greek: the *same* man (attributive), and the man him*self* (predicate).

αὐτός may modify a substantive in the attributive position, and it is translated "same."*

προσηύξατο **τὸν αὐτὸν λόγον** εἰπών (Mark 14:39); "He prayed saying **the same word**."

αὐτός may also be used substantivally to mean "same."

Σωκράτης . . . περιεργάζεται . . . **τὰ αὐτὰ** . . . διδάσκων (The Apology III:7-10); "Socrates . . . is being a busy body . . . teaching . . . **the same things**."

ἀπῇα . . . **τῷ αὐτῷ** (The Apology VII:34); "I departed . . . for **the same reason**."

Declension of Ἰησοῦς

The declension of Ἰησοῦς, "Jesus," is:

Nom.	Ἰησοῦς
Gen.	Ἰησοῦ
Dat.	Ἰησοῦ
Acc.	Ἰησοῦν
Voc.	Ἰησοῦ

The Article Continued

The definite article often modifies proper names; however, it is not translated into English.

γέγραπται ἐν **τῷ Ἡσαΐᾳ** (Mark 1:2); "It is written in **Isaiah**."

In the New Testament the article quite frequently modifies the noun "God," but it is not translated.

εἰσῆλθεν εἰς τὸν οἶκον **τοῦ θεοῦ** (Mark 2:26); "He went into the house of **God**."

In certain contexts the definite article may indicate possession.

λέγει τῷ ἀνθρώπῳ, Ἔκτεινον **τὴν** χεῖρα (Mark 3:5); "He said to the man, 'Stretch out **your** hand.'"

τούτῳ **τὸν** νοῦν προσέχειν (The Apology I:39); "To this direct **your** mind."

Vocabulary

---

* In English the words *self* and *same* stand in the same position as they do in Greek: the *same* man (attributive), and the man him*self* (predicate).

1. αὐτός, ή, ό, third person   he, she, it   (automatic)
    personal pronoun
2. γάρ, postpositive conjunction   for
3. δαιμόνιον, ου, τό   demon or an inferior (demon)
    divine being
4. ἐγώ, first personal   I   (ego)
    personal pronoun
5. ἐκεῖ, adverb   there
6. Ἰησοῦς, οῦ, ὁ   Jesus
7. καθώς, adverb   just as
8. οὖν, postpositive conjunction   then or therefore
9. οὕτως, adverb   thus or so
10. νῦν, adverb   now
11. σύ, second person   you
    personal pronoun
12. τότε, adverb   then
13. ἄρχω, ἄρξω, ἦρξα, --, --, --, rule [the middle voice means "begin"], [active and middle voices take the genitive], (anarch)
14. γίγνομαι or γίνομαι, γενήσομαι, ἐγενόμην, γέγονα, γεγένημαι, ἐγενήθην, become, happen, or am [γίνομαι may be copulative]
15. δύναμαι ["α" occurrs in the present instead of "ε" or "ο"], δυνήσομαι, --,--, δεδύνημαι, ἐδυνήθην, able, (dynamite)
16. ἔρχομαι, ἐλεύσομαι, ἦλθον, ἐλήλυθα, --, --, come or go
17. πίνω, πίομαι, ἔπιον, πέπωκα, πέπομαι, ἐπόθην, drink, (symposium)
18. πορεύομαι, πορεύσομαι, ἐπορευσάμην, --, πεπόρευμαι, ἐπορεύθην, go, (pore)

Translation

1. τότε ἐγὼ ἐλεύσομαι, σὺ γὰρ ἔρχῃ νῦν.
2. ἡ αὐτὴ γίνεται ἀγαθὴ φωνὴ αὐτῇ τῇ ἐκκλησίᾳ.
3. τὰ αὐτὰ δαιμόνια ἐπορεύθη ἐκεῖ· οὕτως πορεύσεσθε αὐτοῖς.
4. αὐτοὶ οὖν ἐρχόμεθα ἐκεῖ ἀλλὰ ἐγὼ αὐτὸς οὐκ ἄρχομαι τοῦ ἔργου.

Mark 1:1*

Ἀρχὴ (ἀρχή, ῆς, ἡ, beginning) τοῦ εὐαγγελίου Ἰησοῦ Χριστοῦ (Χριστός, οῦ, ὁ, Christ) υἱοῦ θεοῦ.

2 Καθὼς γέγραπται (perf. pass. ind. 3 s. of γράφω) ἐν ("in" this preposition is followed by the dative case) τῷ Ἡσαΐᾳ (Ἡσαΐας, ου, ὁ, Isaiah) τῷ προφήτῃ, Ἰδοὺ (behold) ἀποστέλλω (pres. act. ind. 1 s., send) τὸν ἄγγελόν μου πρὸ ("before" this preposition is followed by the genitive case) προσώπου σου, ὅς (who) κατασκευάσει (κατασκευάζω, prepare) τὴν ὁδόν σου· 3 φωνὴ βοῶντος ("of one who is crying") ἐν (in) τῇ ἐρήμῳ, Ἑτοιμάσατε (prepare) τὴν ὁδόν κυρίου, εὐθείας ("straight" translate after the next word) ποιεῖτε (make) τὰς τρίβους (τρίβος, ου, ἡ, path) αὐτοῦ. 4 ἐγένετο Ἰωάννης (Ἰωάννης, ου, ὁ, John) βαπτίζων (baptizing) ἐν (in) τῇ ἐρήμῳ καὶ κηρύσσων (preaching) βάπτισμα (baptism) μετανοίας (μετάνοια, ας, ἡ, repentance) εἰς ἄφεσιν (the two preceding words are translated "unto forgiveness") ἁμαρτιῶν. 5 καὶ ἐξεπορεύετο πρὸς αὐτὸν πᾶσα ἡ Ἰουδαία χώρα καὶ οἱ Ἱεροσολυμῖται πάντες, (translate the preceding words in verse 5: "And all the Judaean country and all the Jerusalemites were going out to him,") καὶ ἐβαπτίζοντο ὑπ' (ὑπό) αὐτοῦ ἐν (in) τῷ Ἰορδάνῃ (Ἰορδάνης, ου, ὁ, Jordan) ποταμῷ (ποταμός, οῦ, ὁ, river) ἐξομολογούμενοι (confessing) τὰς ἁμαρτίας αὐτῶν.

John 8:21

ἐγὼ ὑπάγω (ὑπάγω, go) καὶ ζητήσετέ (ζητέω, seek) με . . . ὅπου (where) ἐγὼ ὑπάγω ὑμεῖς οὐ δύνασθε (δύναμαι, able) ἐλθεῖν (to come).

II Cor. 10:1

---

* The passages from the gospel of Mark are from the *The Greek New Testament* (Stuttgart: United Bible Societies, 1968).

I Pet. 4:1

ὑμεῖς τὴν αὐτὴν ἔννοιαν (ἔννοια, ας, ἡ, mind) ὁπλίσασθε (ὁπλίζω 1st Aor. Mid. imperative 2 pl., arm)

III John 12

μεμαρτύρηται (μαρτυρέω, witness) ὑπὸ πάντων (all men) καὶ ὑπὸ αὐτῆς τῆς ἀληθείας.

Chapter XI

Demonstrative, Relative, and Reciprocal Pronouns

Demonstrative Pronouns

A demonstrative pronoun points out persons or things for special attention. The most frequently used demonstratives are ἐκεῖνος, ὅδε, and οὗτος.

Singular

	Masculine	Feminine	Neuter
Nom.	ἐκεῖνος	ἐκείνη	ἐκεῖνο
Gen.	ἐκείνου	ἐκείνης	ἐκείνου
Dat.	ἐκείνῳ	ἐκείνῃ	ἐκείνῳ
Acc.	ἐκεῖνον	ἐκείνην	ἐκεῖνο

Plural

	Masculine	Feminine	Neuter
Nom.	ἐκεῖνοι	ἐκεῖναι	ἐκεῖνα
Gen.	ἐκείνων	ἐκείνων	ἐκείνων
Dat.	ἐκείνοις	ἐκείναις	ἐκείνοις
Acc.	ἐκείνους	ἐκείνας	ἐκεῖνα

Singular

	Masculine	Feminine	Neuter
Nom.	ὅδε	ἥδε	τόδε
Gen.	τοῦδε	τῆσδε	τοῦδε
Dat.	τῷδε	τῇδε	τῷδε
Acc.	τόνδε	τήνδε	τόδε

Plural

	Masculine	Feminine	Neuter
Nom.	οἵδε	αἵδε	τάδε
Gen.	τῶνδε	τῶνδε	τῶνδε
Dat.	τοῖσδε	ταῖσδε	τοῖσδε
Acc.	τούσδε	τάσδε	τάδε

Except for the accent on the nominatives of the masculine and feminine, the declention of ὅδε is nothing more than the definite article with δε as a suffix.

	Masculine	Singular Feminine	Neuter
Nom.	οὗτος	αὕτη	τοῦτο
Gen.	τούτου	ταύτης	τούτου
Dat.	τούτῳ	ταύτῃ	τούτῳ
Acc.	τοῦτον	ταύτην	τοῦτο
		Plural	
Nom.	οὗτοι	αὗται	ταῦτα
Gen.	τούτων	τούτων	τούτων
Dat.	τούτοις	ταύταις	τούτοις
Acc.	τούτους	ταύτας	ταῦτα

In this declension αυ is in the penult when the ultima has an "α" or an "η;" ου is in the penult when the ultima has an "ο" or an "ω."

When a demonstrative modifies a substantive, it stands in the predicate position.

ἀγοράζει τὸν ἀγρὸν ἐκεῖνον (Matt. 13:44); "He bought **that field.**"

οὗτος ὁ λαὸς ... με τιμᾷ (Mark 7:6); "**This people** ... honor me."

πρέποι ... τῇδε τῇ ἡλικίᾳ (The Apology I:23); "It would not be fitting ... **at this age.**"

The demonstrative may also be used as a substantive. The gender and number usually should be indicated in translation.

ἐκείνη ... ἀπήγγειλεν (Mark 16:10); "**That woman** ... reported."

τίς ἡ σοφία ἡ δοθεῖσα τούτῳ (Mark 6:2); "What is the wisdom that is given **to this man?**"

λέγω ... τόδε (The Apology XXIX:11); "I speak ... **this (word).**"

When οὗτος and ἐκεῖνος are contrasted in meaning, οὗτος refers to what is near, and ἐκεῖνος to what is remote.

κατέβη οὗτος δεδικαιωμένος εἰς τὸν οἶκον αὐτοῦ παρ' ἐκεῖνον (Luke 18:14); "**This man** went down to his house justified rather than **that man.**"

Relative Pronoun

The relative pronoun is declined:

Singular

	Masculine	Feminine	Neuter
Nom.	ὅς	ἥ	ὅ
Gen.	οὗ	ἧς	οὗ
Dat.	ᾧ	ᾗ	ᾧ
Acc.	ὅν	ἥν	ὅ

Plural

	Masculine	Feminine	Neuter
Nom.	οἵ	αἵ	ἅ
Gen.	ὧν	ὧν	ὧν
Dat.	οἷς	αἷς	οἷς
Acc.	οὕς	ἅς	ἅ

A relative pronoun functions as a pronoun and as a connecting word. It is a connective in that it relates the dependent clause which it introduces to a substantive. This substantive is its antecedent. The antecedent governs the gender and number of the relative pronoun. The use of the relative in its clause determines its case.

>   ἀποστέλλω τὸν **ἄγγελόν** ... **ὅς** κατασκευάσει τὴν ὁδόν σου (Mark 1:2); "I am sending the **messenger** ... , **who** will prepare your way."

ὅς is the subject of κατασκευάσει; thus it is in the nominative case. The masculine singular noun ἄγγελον is its antecedent; hence, ὅς also is masculine singular.

>   ἐποίησεν **δώδεκα, οὕς** καὶ ἀποστόλους ὠνόμασεν (Mark 3:14); "He appointed **twelve, whom** he also named apostles."

Since οὕς is the object of ὠνόμασεν, it is in the accusative. The antecedent δώδεκα is masculine plural; thus οὕς is masculine plural.

When the case of the antecedent is either genitive or dative, the relative may be attracted to that case.

>   περὶ **πάντων ὧν** ἐποίησεν (Luke 3:19); "Concerning **all things which** he did."

ὧν is the direct object of ἐποίησεν, and normally a substantive used as the direct object of ἐποίησεν would be in the accusative case. Here, because of attraction to its antecedent, ὧν is in the genitive case. The relative, however, is not always attracted to the case of a genitive or dative antecedent.

τότε ὑπέστρεψαν εἰς Ἰερουσαλὴμ ἀπὸ **ὄρους** (genitive neuter singular third declension noun)... ὅ ἐστιν ἐγγύς (Acts 1:12); "Then they returned unto Jerusalem from a **mountain**... **which** is near."

Reflexive Pronoun

The reflexive pronouns are declined as follows:

	First Person Singular		Second Person Singular	
	Masculine	Feminine	Masculine	Feminine
Gen.	ἐμαυτοῦ	ἐμαυτῆς	σεαυτοῦ	σεαυτῆς
Dat.	ἐμαυτῷ	ἐμαυτῇ	σεαυτῷ	σεαυτῇ
Acc.	ἐμαυτόν	ἐμαυτήν	σεαυτόν	σεαυτήν

	Third Person Singular		
	Masculine	Feminine	Neuter
Gen.	ἑαυτοῦ	ἑαυτῆς	ἑαυτοῦ
Dat.	ἑαυτῷ	ἑαυτῇ	ἑαυτῷ
Acc.	ἑαυτόν	ἑαυτήν	ἑαυτό

	First, Second, and Third Person Plural		
Gen.	ἑαυτῶν	ἑαυτῶν	ἑαυτῶν
Dat.	ἑαυτοῖς	ἑαυταῖς	ἑαυτοῖς
Acc.	ἑαυτούς	ἑαυτάς	ἑαυτά

The reflexive pronoun refers to the subject of its clause; consequently, there is no nominative.

ἔδοξα **ἐμαυτῷ** (Acts 26:9); "I thought **to myself**."

ὕπαγε **σεαυτὸν** δεῖξον (Mark 1:44); "Go show **yourself**."

οὐ μισεῖ τὸν πατέρα **ἑαυτοῦ** (Luke 14:26); "He does not hate **his own** father."

βλέπετε... **ἑαυτούς** (Mark 13:9); "See... **yourselves**."

Reciprocal Pronouns

The reciprocal pronoun is declined:

	Masculine	Feminine	Neuter
Gen.	ἀλλήλων	ἀλλήλων	ἀλλήλων
Dat.	ἀλλήλοις	ἀλλήλαις	ἀλλήλοις
Acc.	ἀλλήλους	ἀλλήλας	ἄλληλα

This pronoun indicates that there is an interchange between members of a plural subject.

ἔλεγον πρὸς **ἀλλήλους** (Mark 4:41); "They were speaking to **each other**."

εἰρηνεύετε ἐν **ἀλλήλοις** (Mark 9:50); "Be at peace with **one another**."

ὀφείλετε **ἀλλήλων** νίπτειν τοὺς πόδας (John 13:14); "You ought to wash **one another's** feet."

Although all three genders are declined above, only the masculine gender occurs in the New Testament.

Vocabulary
1. ἀλλήλων, reciprocal pronoun   (parallel)
2. ἕκαστος, η, ον   each
3. ἐκεῖνος, η, ο, demonstrative pronoun   that
4. ἐμαυτοῦ, σεαυτοῦ, ἑαυτοῦ   reflexive pronoun
5. ἐντολή, ῆς, ἡ   commandment
6. ἤδη adverb   already
7. ἱμάτιον, ου, τό   garment
8. καρπός, οῦ, ὁ   fruit   (carpel)
9. ὅδε, ἥδε, τόδε, demonstrative pronoun   this or that
10. ὅς, ἥ, ὅ, relative pronoun   who or which
11. ὅσος, η, ον   as much as or as great as
    [ὅσος is a relative adjective and introduces relative clauses]
12. ὅτε, adverb   when
13. οὗτος, αὕτη, τοῦτο, demonstrative pronoun   this
14. πάλιν, adverb   again
15. πιστός, ή, όν   faithful
16. πλοῖον, ου, τό   boat
17. ὧδε, adverb   here
18. κηρύσσω, κηρύξω, ἐκήρυξα, κεκήρυχα, κεκήρυγμαι, ἐκηρύχθην, preach, (kerygma)

Translation

1. ἥδε οὖν ἡ ἐντολὴ ὧδε ἐκηρύχθη τούτῳ τῷ Ἰησοῦ ὃς ἐγενήθη πιστὸς ἑκάστῳ ὑμῶν.

2. πάλιν ἄρξομαι ἐκείνου τοῦ ἔργου ἐμαυτῷ καὶ οὕτως εὑρήσομεν ταῦτα ἑαυτοῖς.

3. τὰ τέκνα τοῦ δούλου οὗ οἶδε σε ἤδη ἀλλήλοις σεσώκασιν ὅσον καρπὸν φάγονται.

Mark 1:6

καὶ ἦν (was) ὁ Ἰωάννης (Ἰωάννης, ου, ὁ, John) ἐνδεδυμένος (clothed) τρίχας (hair) καμήλου (κάμηλος, ου, ὁ, camel) καὶ ζώνην (ζώνη, ης, ἡ, belt) δερματίνην (δερμάτινος, η, ον, leather) περὶ (around) τὴν ὀσφὺν (loins) αὐτοῦ, καὶ ἐσθίων (eating) ἀκρίδας (locust) καὶ μέλι (honey) ἄγριον (ἄγριος, α, ον, wild). (Translate verse 6: "And John was clothed in camel's hair and a leather belt around his loins, and was eating locust and wild honey.") 7 καὶ ἐκήρυσσεν λέγων (saying), Ἔρχεται ὁ ἰσχυρότερός (ἰσχυρότερος, α, ον, mightier) μου ὀπίσω ("after" this adverb is followed by the genitive case) μου, οὗ οὐκ εἰμὶ (I am) ἱκανὸς (ἱκανός, ἡ, όν, worthy) κύψας (having stooped) λῦσαι (to loose) τὸν ἱμάντα (thong) τῶν ὑποδημάτων (sandals) αὐτοῦ. 8 ἐγὼ ἐβάπτισα ὑμᾶς ὕδατι (in water), αὐτὸς δὲ βαπτίσει ὑμᾶς ἐν πνεύματι ἁγίῳ (translate the preceding prepositional phrase "in the Holy Spirit").

9 Καὶ ἐγένετο ἐν ("in" this preposition is followed by the dative case) ἐκείναις ταῖς ἡμέραις ἦλθεν Ἰησοῦς ἀπὸ (from) Ναζαρὲτ (Nazareth) τῆς Γαλιλαίας (Γαλιλαία, ας, ἡ, Galilee) καὶ ἐβαπτίσθη εἰς ("into" this preposition is followed by the accusative case) τὸν Ἰορδάνην (Ἰορδάνης, ου, ὁ, Jordan) ὑπὸ Ἰωάννου (John). 10 καὶ εὐθὺς (immediately) ἀναβαίνων (coming up) ἐκ (out of) τοῦ ὕδατος (water) εἶδεν σχιζομένους (being divided) τοὺς οὐρανοὺς

καὶ τὸ πνεῦμα (spirit) ὡς (as) περιστερὰν (περιστερά, ᾶς, ἡ, dove) καταβαῖνον (coming down) εἰς (unto) αὐτόν (translate verse 10: "And immediately while coming up out of the water, he saw that the heavens were being divided and that the Spirit as a dove was coming down unto him.").

Acts 2:33

τήν τε (and) ἐπαγγελίαν (ἐπαγγελία, ας, ἡ, promise [object of λαβών]) τοῦ πνεύματος (gen. n. s., Spirit) τοῦ ἁγίου λαβὼν (having received) παρὰ (from) τοῦ πατρὸς (gen. m. s., father) ἐξέχεεν (1st aor. act. ind. 3 s., pour out) τοῦτο ὃ ὑμεῖς βλέπετε.

Acts 3:25

ὑμεῖς ἐστε (2nd person plural of "to be") οἱ υἱοὶ (predicate complement of the preceding verb) τῶν προφητῶν καὶ τῆς διαθήκης (διαθήκη, ης, ἡ, covenant) ἧς διέθετο (made) ὁ θεός.

II Cor. 4:5

οὐ γὰρ ἑαυτοὺς κηρύσσομεν ἀλλὰ Ἰησοῦν Χριστὸν (Χριστός, οῦ, ὁ, Christ) κύριον, ἑαυτοὺς δὲ δούλους ὑμῶν διὰ (because of) Ἰησοῦν.

II Cor. 13:5

οὐκ ἐπιγινώσκετε (ἐπιγινώσκω, understand) ἑαυτοὺς ὅτι (that) Ἰησοῦς Χριστὸς ἐν (in) ὑμῖν;

Chapter XII

Elision

Prepositions

Compound Verbs

Adverbial and Adjectival Prepositional Phrases

Elision

When a relatively unimportant word, such as a preposition, ending in a short vowel immediately precedes a word beginning with a vowel or diphthong, the final vowel of the preceding word is sometimes dropped. And apostrophe marks the omission; for example, ὑπ' αὐτοῦ (Mark 1:5).

If the elided word ends with a κ, π, or τ and the following word has rough breathing, the last letter of the elided word becomes an aspirated letter; that is, ἀπ' becomes ἀφ' and μετ' becomes μεθ'.* So in Mark 2:19 μετ' αὐτῶν is found, but μεθ' ἑαυτῶν is found in Mark 8:14.

Prepositions

Prepositions are indeclinable words that help substantives express the function of their case when the case is genitive, dative, or accusative. Some prepositions are used with only one case, others with two, and some with three. The meaning of the preposition is governed by the case of the noun which it is aiding. Hence, the case that a preposition is used with and its corresponding meaning must be a matter of vocabulary study.

Compound Verbs

Many verbs join with prepositions to form compound verbs. When a compound is formed, one of three things may happen:

---

* There are no prepositions that illustrate the "κ" changing to the "χ."

1. The preposition and the verb may keep their separate meanings: σύν "with" plus ἔρχομαι "go," συνέρχομαι, means "go with."
2. The preposition may intensify the meaning of the verb: γινώσκω "know" plus ἐπί, ἐπιγινώσκω, means "know fully."
3. The meaning of the compound verb may differ considerably from the meaning of the simple verb: γινώσκω "know" plus ἀνά, ἀναγινώσκω, means "read."

How the meaning of the simple verb will be affected by compounding is a matter of vocabulary study.

Elision* occurs in compound verbs without an apostrophe; that is, διέρχομαι stands for the compound of διά and ἔρχομαι. The augment and reduplication precede the simple verb form rather than the compound; for example, ἐξῆλθον not ἤξελθον and ἀπολέλυκα not ἠπόλυκα. The accent cannot precede the augment or reduplication: ἐξῆλθον not ἔξηλθον.

Many verbs form compounds; but few, if any, appear more often in compounds than ἔρχομαι: ἀπέρχομαι "go from," διέρχομαι "go through," εἰσέρχομαι "go into," ἐξέρχομαι "go out," παρέρχομαι "go by," προέρχομαι "go before," προσέρχομαι "go to," and συνέρχομαι "go with."

The preposition in a compound verb may be repeated after the verb; for example, ἐξῆλθεν ἐξ αὐτοῦ (Mark 1:26); "It came **out of** him." The preposition is not repeated in translation.

Prepositional Phrases

Prepositional phrases are adverbial or adjectival. When the phrase is in the attributive position it is adjectival.

> αἱ **περὶ τὰ λοίπα** ἐπιθυμίαι . . . συμπνίγουσιν τὸν λόγον (Mark 4:19); "The desires **for the remaining things** . . . choke the word."
>
> μάρτυρα ὑμῖν παρέχομαι τὸν θεὸν **τὸν ἐν Δελφοῖς** (The Apology V:25-26); "I shall present to you a witness, the god **in Delphi**."

The adjectival prepositional phrase may be substantival.

> κατεδίωξεν αὐτὸν Σίμων καὶ οἱ **μετ' αὐτοῦ** (Mark 1:36); "Simon and **the men with him** searched for him."

---

* Even though the prepositions περί and πρό end with vowels, they never elide: περιέρχομαι and προέρχομαι.

The adverbial prepositional phrase occurs more often than the adjectival and is easily identified.

καθὼς γέγραπται **ἐν τῷ** Ἡσαΐᾳ τῷ προφήτῃ (Mark 1:2); "Just as it is written **in Isaiah** the prophet."

The distinction between the adverbial and adjectival should be reflected in translation even if it necessitates using a relative clause.

αἱ δυνάμεις **αἱ ἐν τοῖς οὐρανοῖς** σαλευθήσονται (Mark 13:25); "The powers **which are in heaven** will be shaken."

ὅτε δὲ ἀνέβη Πέτρος εἰς Ἰερουσαλήμ, διεκρίνοντο πρὸς* αὐτὸν οἱ ἐκ περιτομῆς (Acts 11:2); "And when Peter went up unto Jerusalem, **the men who were of the circumcision** were disputing with him."

Vocabulary

1. ἀνά, prep. with acc. **up** (analysis)
2. ἀπό, prep. with gen. **from** (apostasy)
3. διά, prep. with gen. **through**, with acc. **because of** (diameter)
4. ἐκ [before vowels ἐξ], prep. with gen. **out of** (exodus)
5. εἰς, prep. with acc. **into** or **unto** (eisegesis)
6. ἐν, prep. with dat. **in** or **on** (enthusiasm)
7. ἐπί, prep. with gen. **on**, with dat. **at**, with acc. **to** (epiphenomenon)
8. κατά, prep. with gen. **down**, with acc. **according to** (cataclysm)
9. μετά, prep. with gen. **with**, with acc. **after** (metaphysics)
10. παρά, prep. with gen. **from**, with dat. **by**, with acc. **beside** (parallel)
11. περί, prep. with gen. **concerning**, with acc. **around** (perimeter)
12. πρό, prep. with gen. **before** (prologue)
13. πρός, prep. with dat. **at**, with acc. **to** (proselyte)
14. σύν, prep. with dat. **with** (syntax)
15. ὑπέρ, prep. with gen. **in behalf of**, with acc. **above** (hypercritical)
16. ὑπό, prep. with gen. **by**, with acc. **under** (hypodermic)
17. ἀπολύω, ἀπολύσω, ἀπέλυσα, ἀπολέλυκε, ἀπολέλυμαι, ἀπελύθην, **release**
18. προσεύχομαι, προσεύξομαι, προσηυξάμην, --, --, --, **pray** (euchology)

---

* πρός is translated "with" in this verse. This is not the translation given in the vocabulary; however, most prepositions have a variety of meanings, far too many to list them all in a beginning grammar.

Translation

1. προσηύχετο ἐν τῇ καρδίᾳ πρὸς τῷ καιρῷ ὁ μετὰ τοῦ Ἰησοῦ τοῦ αὐτοῦ ὁ ἀδελφός μου.

2. αὕτη ἐξῆλθεν ἐκ τοῦ ἐν τῇ ἐρήμῳ οἴκου εἰς τὴν βασιλείαν σου μετ' ἀγγέλου δι' ἀγάπην.

3. μεθ' ἡμέραν τότε οἱ σὺν τῷ δαιμονίῳ εἰσελεύσονται τὸν πονηρὸν τόπον σὺν τοῖς δούλοις ὑμῶν δι' ἁμαρτιῶν αὐτῶν.

Mark 1:11

καὶ φωνὴ ἐγένετο ἐκ τῶν οὐρανῶν, Σὺ εἶ (you are) ὁ υἱός μου ὁ ἀγαπητός, ἐν σοὶ εὐδόκησα (εὐδοκέω, take delight).

12 Καὶ εὐθὺς (immediately) τὸ πνεῦμα (Spirit) αὐτὸν ἐκβάλλει (compound verb of ἐκ and βάλλω) εἰς τὴν ἔρημον. 13 καὶ ἦν (he was) ἐν τῇ ἐρήμῳ τεσσαράκοντα ("forty" acc. fem. pl.) ἡμέρας πειραζόμενος (being tempted) ὑπὸ τοῦ Σατανᾶ ("Satan" gen. case), καὶ ἦν (he was) μετὰ τῶν θηρίων (θηρίον, ου, τό, wild animal), καὶ οἱ ἄγγελοι διηκόνουν (imp. act. ind. 3 pl., provide) αὐτῷ.

14 Μετὰ δὲ τὸ παραδοθῆναι τὸν Ἰωάννην (translate the preceding words in verse 14 "and after John was arrested") ἦλθεν ὁ Ἰησοῦς εἰς τὴν Γαλιλαίαν (Γαλιλαία, ας, ἡ, Galilee) κηρύσσων (preaching) τὸ εὐαγγέλιον τοῦ θεοῦ 15 καὶ λέγων (saying) ὅτι (before a direct quotation ὅτι is not translated) Πεπλήρωται (perf. pass. ind. 3 s., fulfill) ὁ καιρὸς καὶ ἤγγικεν (perf. act. ind. 3 s., draw near) ἡ βασιλεία τοῦ θεοῦ· μετανοεῖτε (repent) καὶ πιστεύετε (believe) ἐν τῷ εὐαγγελίῳ.

Phil. 3:9

εὑρεθῶ (I may be found) ἐν αὐτῷ, μὴ (not) ἔχων (having) ἐμὴν (my) δικαιοσύνην τὴν ἐκ νόμου ἀλλὰ τὴν διὰ πίστεως (gen. noun, faith) Χριστοῦ (Χριστός, οῦ, ὁ, Christ), τὴν ἐκ θεοῦ δικαιοσύνην.

Rom. 4:14

εἰ (since) γὰρ οἱ ἐκ νόμου κληρονόμοι (κληρονόμος, ου, ὁ, heir), κεκένωται (κενόω, make vain) ἡ πίστις (nom. noun, faith).

Acts 11:2

διεκρίνοντο (διακρίνω, take issue) πρὸς αὐτὸν οἱ ἐκ περιτομῆς (περιτομή, ῆς, ἡ, circumcision).

Luke 2:39

ἐτέλεσαν (τελέω, fulfill) πάντα (all) τὰ κατὰ τὸν νόμον κυρίου.

Chapter XIII

Contract Verbs
Possessive Adjectives

Contract Verbs

A verb whose present tense stem ends with an α, ε, or ο is a contract verb: ἐρωτάω, λαλέω, and πληρόω. When the contract verb is conjugated in the present system, the stem vowel and the variable vowel contract and form a new vowel or diphthong. The following chart gives the contractions that may occur.

	ε	η	ο	ω	ει	ῃ	ου	οι
α	α	α	ω	ω	ᾳ	ᾳ	ω	ω
ε	ει	η	ου	ω	ει	ῃ	ου	οι
ο	ου	ω	ου	ω	οι	οι	ου	οι

The rules of accent for the regular verb also apply for the contract verb; however, accenting precedes contraction. If the accent falls on a vowel that is contracted, the accent stays on the new vowel; for example, λαλέει becomes λαλεῖ. After contraction, the rules for kind of accent are applicable. The ultima has a circumflex when it is accented. In the vocabulary the contract verb is given in its uncontracted form, but in literature it is contracted: ἐν παραβολαῖς αὐτοῖς λαλῶ (Matthew 13:13).

Study the present tense system of λαλέω.*

Present Active Indicative

	Singular			Plural		
1.	λαλέω	=	λαλῶ	λαλέομεν	=	λαλοῦμεν
2.	λαλέεις	=	λαλεῖς	λαλέετε	=	λαλεῖτε
3.	λαλέει	=	λαλεῖ	λαλέουσι (ν)	=	λαλοῦσι (ν)

_____
* See page 170 ff. for the conjugations of the "α" and "ο" contract verbs.

Present Middle and Passive Indicative

	Singular			Plural		
1.	λαλέομαι	=	λαλοῦμαι	λαλεόμεθα	=	λαλούμεθα
2.	λαλέῃ	=	λαλῇ	λαλέεσθε	=	λαλεῖσθε
3.	λαλέεται	=	λαλεῖται	λαλέονται	=	λαλοῦνται

Imperfect Active Indicative

	Singular			Plural		
1.	ἐλάλεον	=	ἐλάλουν	ἐλαλέομεν	=	ἐλαλοῦμεν
2.	ἐλάλεες	=	ἐλάλεις	ἐλαλέετε	=	ἐλαλεῖτε
3.	ἐλάλεε(ν)	=	ἐλάλει(ν)	ἐλάλεον	=	ἐλάλουν

Imperfect Middle and Passive Indicative

	Singular			Plural		
1.	ἐλαλεόμην	=	ἐλαλούμην	ἐλαλεόμεθα	=	ἐλαλούμεθα
2.	ἐλαλέου	=	ἐλαλοῦ	ἐλαλέεσθε	=	ἐλαλεῖσθε
3.	ἐλαλέετο	=	ἐλαλεῖτο	ἐλαλέοντο	=	ἐλαλοῦντο

Except in the present tense system, the contract verb is quite similar to the regular "ω" verb. However, when the tense suffix is added, the contract vowel normally lengthens; for example, λαλήσω, ἐλάλησα, λελάληκα, λελάλημαι, ἐλαλήθην.* But there are enough irregularities that the principle parts of the contract verb must also be a matter of vocabulary study; for example, καλέω, καλέσω, ἐκάλεσα, κέκληκα, κέκλημαι, ἐκλήθην.

Possessive Adjectives

The possessive adjectives are the following:

ἐμός, ή, όν	first person singular
ἡμέτερος, α, ον	first person plural
σός, ή, όν	second person plural
ὑμέτερος, α, ον	second person plural
ἴδιος, α, ον	third person singular and plural

These adjectives are declined like ἀγαθός and ἅγιος. The possessive adjective, like other adjectives, must agree in case, gender, and number with the word it

---

* In this grammar the vocabularies have over forty contract verbs. Of these over thirty are "ε" contracts.

modifies. ἴδιος, for all intents and purposes, is interchangeable in meaning with the reflexive pronoun.

Study the following examples:

ὁ λόγος ὁ **ἐμὸς** οὐ χωρεῖ ἐν ὑμῖν (John 8:37) "**My** word is not progressing in you."

εἰς τὴν **ἡμετέραν** διδασκαλίαν ἐγράφη (Romans 15:4); "For **our** instruction it was written."

οἱ δὲ **σοὶ** μαθηταὶ οὐ νηστεύουσιν (Mark 2:18); "But **your** disciples are not fasting."

ἐν τῷ νόμῳ δὲ τῷ **ὑμετέρῳ** γέγραπται (John 8:17); "And in **your** law it is written."

τί . . . τὴν δὲ δοκὸν τὴν ἐν τῷ **ἰδίῳ** ὀφθαλμῷ οὐ κατανοεῖς (Luke 6:41); "But . . . why do you not consider the mote in **your own** eye?"

τοῖς **ἰδίοις** μαθηταῖς ἐπέλυεν πάντα (Mark 4:34); "He was explaining all things to **his own** disciples."

ἀκούομεν . . . τῇ **ἰδίᾳ** διαλέκτῳ (Acts 2:8); "We hear . . . in **our own** dialect."

Vocabulary

1. διδάσκαλος, ου, ὁ   teacher   (διδάσκω)
2. ἐμός, ή, όν   my
3. εὐθύς, adverb   immediately
4. ἡμέτερος, α, ον   our
5. θρόνος, ου, ὁ   throne   (throne)
6. ἴδιος, α, ον   one's own   (idiosyncrasy)
7. ὅτι, conjunction   that or because
8. σάββατον, ου, τό   sabbath
   [the dative plural is σάββασι (ν); sometimes a plural form of σάββατον is used to refer to a single sabbath]
9. σός, ή, όν   your
10. ὑμέτερος, α, ον   your
11. δέχομαι, δέξομαι, ἐδεξάμην, --, δέδεγμαι, ἐδέχθην, receive
12. δοξάζω, δοξάσω, ἐδόξασα, δεδόξακα, δεδόξασμαι, ἐδοξάσθην, glorify
13. ἐπερωτάω, ἐπερωτήσω, ἐπηρώτησα, ἐπηρώτηκα, ἐπηρώτημαι, ἐπηρωτήθην, ask or question
14. ἐρωτάω, ἐρωτήσω, ἠρώτησα, ἠρώτηκα, ἠρώτημαι, ἠρωτήθην, ask

15. ζητέω, ζητήσω, ἐζήτησα, --, --, --, seek
16. καλέω, καλέσω, ἐκάλεσα, κέκληκα, κέκλημαι, ἐκλήθην, call
17. κράζω, κράξω, ἔκραξα or ἔκραγον, κέκραγα, --, --, cry
18. λαλέω, λαλήσω, ἐλάλησα, λελάληκα, λελάλημαι, ἐλαλήθην, say or talk
19. πληρόω, πληρώσω, ἐπλήρωσα, πεπλήρωκα, πεπλήρωμαι, ἐπληρώθην, fulfill
20. ποιέω, ποιήσω, ἐποίησα, πεποίηκα, πεποίημαι, ἐποιήθην, do (poet)
21. συνάγω, συνάξω, συνήγαγον, συνῆχα, συνῆγμαι, συνήχθην, gather together (synagogue)

Translation

1. ἐν σάββασιν ἐζήτουν οἱ ἐμοὶ διδάσκαλοι τὰ ἴδια ἀλλὰ οὐ λαλῶ περὶ αὐτῶν.

2. ὁ ἡμέτερος ἄνθρωπος ὁ ἐν τῷ θρόνῳ τὸν νόμον ἐπλήρουν καὶ ποιήσει ἀγαθὰ τῷ ἰδίῳ λαῷ ἀλλὰ οἱ ὑμέτεροι νόμοι ἐπερωτῶνται ὑπ' αὐτοῦ.

Mark 1:16

Καὶ παράγων (passing along) παρὰ τὴν θάλασσαν τῆς Γαλιλαίας (Γαλιλαία, ας, ἡ, Galilee) εἶδεν Σίμωνα (Simon) καὶ Ἀνδρέαν (Ἀνδρέας, ου, ὁ, Andrew) τὸν ἀδελφὸν Σίμωνος (of Simon) ἀμφιβάλλοντας (casting a net) ἐν τῇ θαλάσσῃ· ἦσαν (they were) γὰρ ἁλιεῖς (fishermen). 17 καὶ εἶπεν αὐτοῖς ὁ Ἰησοῦς, Δεῦτε (come) ὀπίσω ("after" this adverb is followed by the genitive case) μου, καὶ ποιήσω ὑμᾶς γενέσθαι (to become) ἁλιεῖς (fishermen) ἀνθρώπων. 18 καὶ εὐθὺς ἀφέντες (having left) τὰ δίκτυα (δίκτυον, ου, τό, net) ἠκολούθησαν (ἀκολουθέω, follow) αὐτῷ. 19 καὶ προβὰς (having gone) ὀλίγον (a little farther) εἶδεν Ἰάκωβον (Ἰάκωβος, ου, ὁ, James) τὸν τοῦ Ζεβεδαίου (translate the three preceding words "the son of Zebedee") καὶ Ἰωάννην (Ἰωάννης, ου, ὁ, John) τὸν ἀδελφὸν αὐτοῦ, καὶ αὐτοὺς ἐν τῷ πλοίῳ καταρτίζοντας (mending) τὰ δίκτυα (net), 20 καὶ εὐθὺς ἐκάλεσεν αὐτούς. καὶ ἀφέντες (having left) τὸν πατέρα (father) αὐτῶν Ζεβεδαῖον (Ζεβεδαῖος, ου, ὁ,

Zebedee) ἐν τῷ πλοίῳ μετὰ τῶν μισθωτῶν (μισθωτός, οῦ, ὁ, laborer) ἀπῆλθον ὀπίσω (after) αὐτοῦ.

21 Καὶ εἰσπορεύονται (compound of εἰς and πορεύομαι) εἰς Καφαρναούμ (Capernaum). καὶ εὐθὺς τοῖς σάββασιν εἰσελθὼν (having entered) εἰς τὴν συναγωγὴν (συναγωγή, ῆς, ἡ, synagogue) ἐδίδασκεν. 22 καὶ ἐξεπλήσσοντο ("be amazed" compound verb of ἐκ and πλήσσομαι) ἐπὶ τῇ διδαχῇ (διδαχή, ῆς, ἡ, teaching) αὐτοῦ, ἦν (he was) γὰρ διδάσκων (teaching) αὐτοὺς ὡς (as) ἐξουσίαν ἔχων (having) καὶ οὐχ ὡς (as) οἱ γραμματεῖς (scribes).

I Cor. 16:17
τὸ ὑμέτερον ὑστέρημα (acc. n. s., lack) οὗτοι ἀνεπλήρωσαν (ἀναπληρόω, fill).

II Tim. 4:15
λίαν (adv., exceedingly) γὰρ ἀντέστη (ἀνθίστημι, he resisted) τοῖς ἡμετέροις λόγοις.

John 5:18
διὰ τοῦτο οὖν μᾶλλον (more) ἐζήτουν αὐτὸν οἱ Ἰουδαῖοι (Ἰουδαῖος, α, ον, Jew).

II Tim. 4:3
ἀλλὰ κατὰ τὰς ἰδίας ἐπιθυμίας (ἐπιθυμία, ας, ἡ, desire) ἑαυτοῖς ἐπισωρεύσουσιν (ἐπισωρεύω, collect) διδασκάλους.

Chapter XIV

Dative of Location

Indirect Discourse

μι Verbs

Dative of Location

The dative case without a preposition may express location. This use answers the question "where" or "when." The following examples answer "when."

καὶ εὐθὺς **τοῖς σάββασιν** ... ἐδίδασκεν (Mark 1:21); "And immediately **on the Sabbath** ... he was teaching."

καὶ **τῇ πρώτῃ ἡμέρᾳ** ... λέγουσιν αὐτῷ οἱ μαθηταὶ αὐτοῦ (Mark 14:12); "And **on the first day** ... his disciples were speaking to him."

These examples tell "where."*

οἱ δὲ ἄλλοι μαθηταὶ **τῷ πλοιαρίῳ** ἦλθον (John 21:8); "And the other disciples came **in the little boat**."

ἐγὼ ἐβάπτισα ὑμᾶς **ὕδατι** (Mark 1:8); "I myself baptized you **in water**."

Indirect Discourse

An indirect quotation or discourse repeats a speech or thought in substance, but usually with some change in its form. The Bible contains the following direct quote:

Σὺ εἶ [second person present of εἰμι, "to be"] ὁ υἱός μου ὁ ἀγαπητός (Mark 1:11); "You yourself are my beloved son."

As an indirect quote this statement would have been:

ὁ θεὸς εἶπεν ὅτι αὐτὸς ἐστιν [third person present of εἰμι, "to be"] ὁ υἱὸς αὐτοῦ ὁ ἀγαπητός, "God said that he himself was his beloved son."

---

* It is possible to interpret both of these illustrations as datives of means (Chapter VII).

Note that in the Greek sentence the indirect discourse retains the tense (ἐστιν) of the direct discourse (εἶ), but in the English sentence the present tense of the direct discourse (are) becomes the past tense (was). In Greek, regardless of the tense, the indirect discourse retains the tense of the direct discourse. In English the tense of the verb makes the following changes when the indirect discourse follows a verb with a secondary tense:

   Direct: You said, "I see you."
   Indirect: You said that you saw me.
   Direct: You said, "I shall see you."
   Indirect: You said that you would see me.
   Direct: You said, "I have seen you."
   Indirect: You said that you had seen me.
   Direct: You said, "I saw you."
   Indirect: You said that you have seen me.

μι verbs

In addition to the "ω" verbs, there are a few important verbs whose present active indicative first person singular ending is μι. The μι verbs may divided into three principal classes:

1. The νυμι class, in which νυ occurs between the stem and the ending; for example, δείκ-**νυ**-μι.
2. The reduplicating present class, in which the initial consonant is reduplicated with an iota: the present of δο is δί-δω-μι.
3. The root class, in which the personal endings are added directly to the root. Verbs of this class have irregular inflection; thus, the conjugation of each of these verbs is a matter of separate study.

εἰμι, "to be," occurs more frequently than any other verb of the root class. Its root is ἐς, but the only conjugation in which the root is observable in each form is the future.

	Present Indicative	
	Singular	Plural
1.	εἰμι	ἐσμεν
2.	εἶ	ἐστε
3.	ἐστι (ν)	εἰσι (ν)

Imperfect Indicative

	Singular	Plural
1.	ἤμην	ἦμεν
2.	ἦς	ἦτε
3.	ἦν	ἦσαν

Future Indicative

	Singular	Plural
1.	ἔσομαι	ἐσόμεθα
2.	ἔσῃ	ἔσεσθε
3.	ἔσται	ἔσονται

Except for εἶ, the forms of the present indicative are enclitics.

εἰμι is a linking verb; hence, it may have a predicate complement which will be in the nominative case.

οὐκ εἰμὶ **ἱκανός** (Mark 1:7); "I am not **worthy**."

εἶ ὁ **υἱός** μου (Mark 1:11); "You are my **son**."

The subject may be distinguished from the predicate complement by the presence of the article.

κύριός ἐστιν **ὁ υἱὸς** τοῦ ἀνθρώπου καὶ τοῦ σαββάτου (Mark 2:28); "**The son** of man is even master of the Sabbath."

θεὸς ἦν ὁ **λόγος** (John 1:1); "**The word** was God."

Vocabulary

1. ἀρχή, ῆς, ἡ — beginning (archaic)
2. ἐνώπιον, adverb followed by the gen., "before"
3. ἔξω, adverb followed by the gen., "outside"
4. ὅπου, relative adverb, "where"
5. πῶς, interrogative adverb, "how"
6. ἀγαπάω, ἀγαπήσω, ἠγάπησα, ἠγάπηκα, ἠγάπημαι, ἠγαπήθην, love
7. αἰτέω, αἰτήσω, ᾔτησα, ᾔτηκα, ᾔτημαι, ᾐτήθην, ask or ask for
8. ἀκολουθέω, ἀκολουθήσω, ἠκολούθησα, ἠκολούθηκα, --, --, [takes the dative], follow, (acolyte)
9. ἀσπάζομαι, ἀσπάσομαι, ἠσπασάμην, --, --, --, greet or salute
10. γεννάω, γεννήσω, ἐγέννησα, γεγέννηκα, γεγέννημαι, ἐγεννήθην, bear or give birth
11. εἰμι, ἔσομαι, am

12. ὁράω, ὄψομαι, --, ἑόρακα or ἑώρακα, ὦμμαι, ὤφθην, see (panorama)
13. παρακαλέω, παρακαλέσω, παρεκάλεσα, παρακέκληκα, παρακέκλημαι, παρεκλήθην, comfort or exhort, (Paraclete)
14. περιπατέω, περιπατήσω, περιεπάτησα, περιπεπάτηκα, --, --, walk, (peripatetics)
15. φέρω, οἴσω, ἤνεγκα or ἤνεγκον, ἐνήνοχα, ἐνήνεγμαι, ἠνέχθην, carry, (Christopher)

Translation

1. τῇ πρώτῃ ὥρᾳ τῆς ἡμέρας ἐλάλησεν ἑτοίμοις λόγοις ὁ προφήτης ὅτι ἡ σὴ ἐκκλησία ἀκολουθεῖ τῷ ἁγίῳ θεῷ ὅπου ἦχεν αὐτὴν καὶ αὐτὴ ἡ ἐκκλησία ἐστιν ἀγαθή.

2. ταῖς καρδίαις αὐτῶν οἱ μετὰ τοῦ ἀποστόλου ἐγίνωσκον ὅτι κύριος τοῦ κόσμου καὶ τοῦ οὐρανοῦ ἔσται ὁ ἀγαπητὸς υἱός.

Mark 1:23

καὶ εὐθὺς ἦν ἐν τῇ συναγωγῇ (συναγωγή, ῆς, ἡ, synagogue) αὐτῶν ἄνθρωπος ἐν πνεύματι ἀκαθάρτῳ (translate the three preceding words "with an unclean spirit"), καὶ ἀνέκραξεν ("cry out" compound verb of ἀνά and κράζω) 24 λέγων (saying), Τί ἡμῖν καὶ σοί (translate the four preceding words "what have we to do with you"), Ἰησοῦ Ναζαρηνέ (Ναζαρηνός, οῦ, ὁ, Nazarene); ἦλθες ἀπολέσαι (to destroy) ἡμᾶς; οἶδά σε τίς (who) εἶ, ὁ ἅγιος τοῦ θεοῦ. 25 καὶ ἐπετίμησεν ("rebuke" compound verb of ἐπί and τιμάω) αὐτῷ ὁ Ἰησοῦς λέγων (saying), Φιμώθητι (be silenced) καὶ ἔξελθε (come out) ἐξ αὐτοῦ. 26 καὶ σπαράξαν (having convulsed) αὐτὸν τὸ πνεῦμα τὸ ἀκάθαρτον (the four preceding words, "the unclean spirit," are the subject of ἐξῆλθεν) καὶ φωνῆσαν φωνῇ μεγάλῃ (translate the three preceding words "having cried with a great voice") ἐξῆλθεν ἐξ αὐτοῦ. 27 καὶ ἐθαμβήθησαν (θαμβέω, astound) ἅπαντες ("all" is the subject of ἐθαμβήθησαν), ὥστε συζητεῖν πρὸς ἑαυτοὺς (translate the four preceding words "with the results that they were disputing with themselves") λέγοντας (saying), Τί (what) ἐστιν τοῦτο; διδαχὴ (διδαχή, ῆς, ἡ, teaching) καινὴ (καινός, ή, όν, new) κατ' ἐξουσίαν· καὶ (even) τοῖς πνεύμασι τοῖς ἀκαθάρτοις ("the unclean spirits" is the object of ἐπιτάσσει) ἐπιτάσσει ("command" compound verb of ἐπί and τάσσω), καὶ ὑπακούουσιν ("obey" compound verb of ὑπό and ἀκούω) αὐτῷ. 28 καὶ ἐξῆλθεν ἡ ἀκοὴ (ἀκοή, ῆς, ἡ, report) αὐτοῦ εὐθὺς πανταχοῦ (everywhere) εἰς ὅλην τὴν περίχωρον (περίχωρος, ου, ἡ, surrounding region) τῆς Γαλιλαίας (Γαλιλαία, ας, ἡ, Galilee).

29 Καὶ εὐθὺς ἐκ τῆς συναγωγῆς (synagogue) ἐξελθόντες (having come out) ἦλθον εἰς τὴν οἰκίαν (οἰκία, ας, ἡ, house) Σίμωνος (of Simon) καὶ Ἀνδρέου (Ἀνδρέας, ου, ὁ, Andrew) μετὰ Ἰακώβου (Ἰάκωβος, ου, ὁ, James) καὶ Ἰωάννου (Ἰωάννης, ου, ὁ, John). 30 ἡ δὲ πενθερὰ (πενθερά, ᾶς, ἡ, mother-in-law) Σίμωνος (of Simon) κατέκειτο (κατάκειμαι, lie) πυρέσσουσα (being feverish), καὶ εὐθὺς λέγουσιν αὐτῷ περὶ αὐτῆς.

John 10:3
τὰ πρόβατα (πρόβατον, ου, τό, sheep) τῆς φωνῆς αὐτοῦ ἀκούει, καὶ τὰ ἴδια πρόβατα φωνεῖ (φωνέω, call) κατ' ὄνομα (acc. noun, name).
John 10:14
ἐγώ εἰμι ὁ ποιμὴν (nom. noun, shepherd) ὁ καλός, καὶ γινώσκω τὰ ἐμὰ καὶ γινώσκουσί με τὰ ἐμά.
Acts 16:17
οὗτοι οἱ ἄνθρωποι δοῦλοι τοῦ θεοῦ τοῦ ὑψίστου (ὕψιστος, η, ον, most high) εἰσίν.

Chapter XV

Reduplicated μι Verbs

The present tense stem of the reduplicated μι verb is formed by repeating the initial consonant of its root with an iota. The roots δο, θε, and στα, are important representatives of this class of verbs.

The μι verbs have the following personal endings:

	Primary Active		Secondary Active	
	Singular	Plural	Singular	Plural
1.	μι	μεν	ν	μεν
2.	ς	τε	ς	τε
3.	σι	ασι	-	σαν

	Primary Mid. and Pass.		Secondary Mid. and Pass	
	Singular	Plural	Singular	Plural
1.	μαι	μεθα	μην	μεθα
2.	σαι	σθε	σο	σθε
3.	ται	νται	το	ντο

In the present, imperfect, and second aorist tenses the personal endings are added directly to the tense stem without a variable vowel. The student should exercise particular care in observing the root vowel (δο, θε, and στα) throughout the conjugations. In the active voice of the present system the vowel is long when the verb is singular but short when the verb is plural. The vowel is short in the middle and passive voices of the present system.

Present System

Present Active Indicative
Singular

1.	δίδωμι	τίθημι	ἵστημι
2.	δίδως	τίθης	ἵστης
3.	δίδωσι (ν)	τίθησι (ν)	ἵστησι (ν)

Plural

1.	δίδομεν	τίθεμεν	ἵσταμεν
2.	δίδοτε	τίθετε	ἵστατε
3.	διδόασι (ν)	τιθέασι (ν)	ἱστᾶσι (ν)

Observe:
1. The reduplicated form of στα was originally σιστα, but the beginning "σ" was later replaced by rough breathing.
2. The third person plural form, ἱστᾶσι, is a contraction of ἱστα and ασι.

Present Middle and Passive Indicative
Singular

1.	δίδομαι	τίθεμαι	ἵσταμαι
2.	δίδοσαι	τίθεσαι	ἵστασαι
3.	δίδοται	τίθεται	ἵσταται

Plural

1.	διδόμεθα	τιθέμεθα	ἱστάμεθα
2.	δίδοσθε	τίθεσθε	ἵστασθε
3.	δίδονται	τίθενται	ἵστανται

Imperfect Active Indicative
Singular

1.	ἐδίδουν	ἐτίθην	ἵστην
2.	ἐδίδους	ἐτίθεις	ἵστης*
3.	ἐδίδου	ἐτίθει	ἵστη

Plural

1.	ἐδίδομεν	ἐτίθεμεν	ἵσταμεν*
2.	ἐδίδοτε	ἐτίθετε	ἵστατε*
3.	ἐδίδοσαν	ἐτίθεσαν	ἵστασαν

Imperfect Middle and Passive Indicative
Singular

1.	ἐδιδόμην	ἐτιθέμην	ἱστάμην
2.	ἐδίδοσο	ἐτίθεσο	ἵστασο
3.	ἐδίδοτο	ἐτίθετο	ἵστατο

---

* These forms are exactly the same as their counterparts in the present tense. The context must indicate the proper translation.

	Plural		
1.	ἐδιδόμεθα	ἐτιθέμεθα	ἱστάμεθα
2.	ἐδίδοσθε	ἐτίθεσθε	ἵστασθε
3.	ἐδίδοντο	ἐτίθεντο	ἵσταντο

Future System

The future active and middle μι verbs are conjugated like the "ω" verbs.

Aorist System

There are first and second aorist conjugations for ἵστημι.*

	First Aorist Active Indicative		Second Aorist Active Indicative	
	Singular	Plural	Singular	Plural
1.	ἔστησα	ἐστήσαμεν	ἔστην	ἔστημεν
2.	ἔστησας	ἐστήσατε	ἔστης	ἔστητε
3.	ἔστησε (ω)	ἔστησαν	ἔστη	ἔστησαν

The first aorist of ἵστημι is transitive;** for example,

λαβὼν παιδίον **ἔστησεν** αὐτὸ ἐν μέσῳ αὐτῶν (Mark 9:36); "After having taken a child he **stood** (caused to stand) him in the midst of them."

The second aorist of ἵστημι is intransitive:

αὐτὸς **ἔστη** ἐν μέσῳ αὐτῶν (Luke 24:36); "He himself **stood** in their midst."

δο and θε have the first aorist forms in the active voice and second aorist in the middle voice. The first and second aorist of these two verbs have the same significance. However, the suffix for the first aorist is κα and not σα.

First Aorist Active Indicative

	Singular	Plural	Singular	Plural
1.	ἔδωκα	ἐδώκαμεν	ἔθηκα	ἐθήκαμεν
2.	ἔδωκας	ἐδώκατε	ἔθηκας	ἐθήκατε
3.	ἔδωκε (ν)	ἔδωκαν	ἔθηκε (ν)	ἔθηκαν

---

* There is no second aorist middle indicative, and the first aorist middle indicative is conjugated like the "ω" verbs.
** A transitive verb has an actor and a receiver of the action. It may have either active, middle, or passive voice. The actor or receiver may be understood. An intransitive complete verb makes a complete statement without the help of any other word.

Second Aorist Middle Indicative

	Singular	Plural	Singular	Plural
1.	ἐδόμην	ἐδόμεθα	ἐθέμην	ἐθέμεθα
2.	ἔδου	ἔδοσθε	ἔθου	ἔθεσθε
3.	ἔδοτο	ἔδοντο	ἔθετο	ἔθεντο

Perfect Active System

The perfect active follows the "ω" conjugation; however, the root vowels warrant special attention: δέδωκα, τέθεικα, and ἔστηκα.

Perfect Middle and Passive Systems

The conjugation of this system also follows the conjugation of the "ω" verb, and again the root vowel should be observed: δέδομαι, τέθειμαι, and ἔσταμαι.

Aorist Passive System

The conjugation of the aorist passive system is the same as the "ω" conjugation, but the root vowels do not change: ἐδόθην, ἐτέθην, and ἐστάθην.

Second Aorist of γινώσκω

In the second aorist, γινώσκω and a few other "ω" verbs follow the μι conjugation in omitting variable vowels. The aorist stem of γινώσκω is γνο.

Second Aorist Active Indicative of γινώσκω

	Singular	Plural
1.	ἔγνων	ἔγνωμεν
2.	ἔγνως	ἔγνωτε
3.	ἔγνω	ἔγνωσαν

Vocabulary

1. λοιπός, ή, όν — remaining
2. μέσος, η, ον — middle (Mesopotamia)
3. πρεσβύτερος, α, ον — elder (Presbyterian)
4. ἀποδίδωμι, ἀποδώσω, ἀπέδωκα, ἀποδέδωκα, ἀποδέδομαι, ἀπεδόθην, give back, [the middle voice means "sell"]
5. ἀφίημι, ἀφήσω, ἀφῆκα, ἀφεῖκα, ἀφεῖμαι, ἀφείθην, leave or forgive, (aphesis)

6. δίδωμι, δώσω, ἔδωκα, δέδωκα, δέδομαι, ἐδόθην, give (antidote)
7. δοκέω, δόξω, ἔδοξα, --, δέδογμαι, --, seem or think, (Docetism)
8. ἵημι, ἥσω, ἧκα, εἷκα, εἷμαι, εἵθην, send or throw
9. ἵστημι, στήσω, ἔστησα or ἔστην, ἔστηκα, ἔσταμαι, ἐστάθην, stand, (ecstasy)
10. κάθημαι, [κάθημαι occurs only in the present and "η" is used instead of "ε" or "ο"], sit
11. μαρτυρέω, μαρτυρήσω, ἐμαρτύρησα, μεμαρτύρηκα, μεμαρτύρημαι, ἐμαρτυρήθην, witness, (martyr)
12. παραδίδωμι, παραδώσω, παρέδωκα, παραδέδωκα, παραδέδομαι, παρεδόθην, deliver or hand over
13. τηρέω, τηρήσω, ἐτήρησα, τετήρηκα, τετήρημαι, ἐτηρήθην, keep
14. τίθημι, θήσω, ἔθηκα, τέθεικα, τέθειμαι, ἐτέθην, put or place, (thesis)
15. φήμι, φήσω, ἔφησα, --, --, --, say (blaspheme)

Translation

1. σὺν ταῖς πρεσβυτέραις ἔστημεν παρὰ τῷ λοιπῷ πλοίῳ τοῦ διδασκάλου ἀλλὰ ἐστήσαμεν τὰ τέκνα ἡμῶν ἐν ἐκείνῳ τῷ ἑτέρῳ πλοίῳ.

2. παρέδωκα γὰρ ἐγὼ ὑμῖν τὰ καλὰ ἃ δέδοταί μοι ὑπὸ τοῦ κυρίου ἡμῶν· ἐθήκατε δὲ αὐτὰ ἔξω τοῦ οἴκου ὑμῶν.

3. ἔγνωσαν οἱ ἀπὸ τῆς ἄλλης ἐκκλησίας ἄνθρωποι ὅτι ὁ υἱὸς ὑμῶν δέδωκε τὰ ἐμὰ ἱμάτια ὑμῖν.

Mark 1:31

καὶ προσελθὼν (having come) ἤγειρεν (he raised) αὐτὴν κρατήσας (having taken hold) τῆς χειρός (hand)· καὶ ἀφῆκεν αὐτὴν ὁ πυρετός (πυρετός, οῦ ὁ, fever), καὶ διηκόνει (imp. act. ind. 3 s., serve) αὐτοῖς. 32 Ὀψίας (ὀψία, ας, ἡ, evening) δὲ γενομένης (translate the three preceding words "and after evening had come"), ὅτε ἔδυ (sec. aor. act. ind. 3 s., set) ὁ ἥλιος (ἥλιος, ου, ὁ, sun), ἔφερον πρὸς αὐτὸν πάντας τοὺς κακῶς ἔχοντας (translate the four preceding words "all who were having it badly") καὶ τοὺς δαιμονιζομένους (who were being demon possessed)· 33 καὶ ἦν ὅλη ἡ πόλις (city) ἐπισυνηγμένη (gathered together) πρὸς τὴν θύραν (θύρα, ας, ἡ, door). 34 καὶ ἐθεράπευσεν (θεραπεύω, heal) πολλοὺς κακῶς ἔχοντας (translate the three preceding words "many who were having it badly") ποικίλαις (ποικίλος, η, ον, all kinds of) νόσοις (νόσος, ου, ἡ, illness), καὶ δαιμόνια πολλὰ (many) ἐξέβαλεν (compound of ἐκ and βάλλω), καὶ οὐκ ἤφιεν ("permit" imp. act. of ἀφίημι) λαλεῖν (to speak) τὰ δαιμόνια, ὅτι ᾔδεισαν (pluperfect of οἶδα) αὐτόν.

35 Καὶ πρωὶ ἔννυχα λίαν ἀναστὰς (translate the four preceding words "very early while still dark having arisen") ἐξῆλθεν καὶ ἀπῆλθεν εἰς ἔρημον τόπον κἀκεῖ (a combination of καί and ἐκεῖ) προσηύχετο. 36 καὶ κατεδίωξεν ("hunt" compound of κατά and διώκω) αὐτὸν Σίμων (Simon) καὶ οἱ μετ' αὐτοῦ, 37 καὶ εὗρον αὐτὸν καὶ λέγουσιν αὐτῷ ὅτι Πάντες (all) ζητοῦσίν σε. 38 καὶ λέγει αὐτοῖς, Ἄγωμεν (let us go) ἀλλαχοῦ (elsewhere) εἰς τὰς ἐχομένας (neighboring) κωμοπόλεις (towns) ἵνα (in order that) καὶ (also) ἐκεῖ κηρύξω (I may preach)· εἰς τοῦτο γὰρ ἐξῆλθον.

Matt. 21:45
ἀκούσαντες (having heard) . . . οἱ φαρισαῖοι (φαρισαῖος, ου, ὁ, Pharisees) τὰς παραβολὰς αὐτοῦ ἔγνωσαν ὅτι περὶ αὐτῶν λέγει.

Acts 6:5,6
ἐξελέξαντο (ἐκλέγω, choose) Στέφανον (Στεπανός, ου, ὁ, Stephen) καὶ Φίλιππον (Φίλιππος, ου, ὁ, Philip) οὓς ἔστησαν ἐνώπιον τῶν ἀποστόλων.

Acts 10:30
καὶ ἰδοὺ (behold) ἀνὴρ (nom. noun, "man") ἔστη ἐνώπιόν μου.

Chapter XVI

μι Verbs of the νυ Class
Third Declension Nouns
Accusative of Extent
Genitive of Time

νυ Verbs

The third class of μι verbs forms its present tense stem by suffixing νυ to the verb root. Like other μι verbs, this class does not use variable vowels.

Present Indicative of δείκνυμι

	Active		Middle and Passive	
	Singular	Plural	Singular	Plural
1.	δείκνυμι	δείκνυμεν	δείκνυμαι	δεικνύμεθα
2.	δείκνυς	δείκνυτε	δείκνυσαι	δείκνυσθε
3.	δείκνυσι (ν)	δεικνύασι (ν)	δείκνυται	δείκνυνται

Imperfect Indicative of δείκνυμι

	Active		Middle and Passive	
	Singular	Plural	Singular	Plural
1.	ἐδείκνυν	ἐδείκνυμεν	ἐδεικνύμην	ἐδεικνύμεθα
2.	ἐδείκνυς	ἐδείκνυτε	ἐδείκνυσο	ἐδείκνυσθε
3.	ἐδείκνυ	ἐδείκνυσαν	ἐδείκνυτο	ἐδείκνυντο

A few verbs of this class whose roots end with υ do not use the νυ suffix, but are conjugated like δείκνυμι; for example, ἀπόλλυμι.

Present Indicative of ἀπόλλυμι

	Active		Middle and Passive	
	Singular	Plural	Singular	Plural
1.	ἀπόλλυμι	ἀπόλλυμεν	ἀπόλλυμαι	ἀπολλύμεθα
2.	ἀπόλλυς	ἀπόλλυτε	ἀπόλλυσαι	ἀπόλλυσθε
3.	ἀπόλλυσι (ν)	ἀπολλύασι (ν)	ἀπόλλυται	ἀπόλλυνται

Imperfect Indicative of ἀπόλλυμι

	Active		Middle and Passive	
	Singular	Plural	Singular	Plural
1.	ἀπώλλυν	ἀπόλλυμεν	ἀπωλλύμην	ἀπωλλύμεθα
2.	ἀπώλλυς	ἀπώλλυτε	ἀπώλλυσο	ἀπώλλυσθε
3.	ἀπώλλυ	ἀπώλλυσαν	ἀπώλλυτο	ἀπώλλυντο

Except in the present tense system, the νυ verbs are conjugated like "ω" verbs. Moreover, even in the present system a few νυ verbs are sometimes conjugated like "ω" verbs. This is the reason that ἀπόλλυμι, ἀνοίγνυμι, and δείκνυμι are given in the vocabulary as both "ω" and μι verbs. Contrast the personal endings of δείκνυμι in these two verses.

τί σημεῖον **δεικνύεις** ["ω" conjugation] ἡμῖν; (John 2:18); "What sign do you **show** us?"

ὁ γὰρ πατὴρ φιλεῖ τὸν υἱὸν καὶ πάντα **δείκνυσιν** [μι conjugation] αὐτῷ (John 5:20); "For the father loves the son and **shows** all things to him."

Third Declension Nouns

Third declension nouns usually use the following endings:

	Singular		
	Mas. & Fem.	All	Neuter
Nom.		--	
Gen.		ος	
Dat.		ι	
Acc.	α		Like the Nom.
Voc.	--		Like the Nom.

	Plural		
	Mas. & Fem.	All	Neuter
Nom.	ες		α
Gen.		ων	
Dat.		σι	
Acc.	ας		Like the Nom.
Voc.		Like the Nom.	

The stem, to which these endings are suffixed, is found by dropping the ος of the genitive singular; that is, the stem of ἄρχων, ἄρχοντος, ὁ, "ruler" is ἀρχοντ. Consequently, both the nominative and genitive singulars must be memorized.

The gender is also a matter of vocabulary study, and the vocative of the masculine and feminine is formed in various ways.

The suffixing of the σι for the dative plural creates the same problems encountered in forming the future and first aorist tenses (Chapter VI). It is usually possible to predict the dative plural form, but the correct spelling is a matter of lexical study.

The declensions of ἄρχων, ἄρχοντος, ὁ and ὄνομα, ὀνόματος, τὸ are as follows:

Singular

Nom.	ἄρχων	ὄνομα
Gen.	ἄρχοντος	ὀνόματος
Dat.	ἄρχοντι	ὀνόματι
Acc.	ἄρχοντα	ὄνομα
Voc.	ἄρχων	ὄνομα

Plural

Nom.	ἄρχοντες	ὀνόματα
Gen.	ἀρχόντων	ὀνομάτων
Dat.	ἄρχουσι (ν)	ὀνόμασι (ν)
Acc.	ἄρχοντας	ὀνόματα
Voc.	ἄρχοντες	ὀνόματα

As in the case of ἄρχων and ὄνομα, third declension nouns follow the normal rules of noun accent. An exception to this is the monosyllabic noun. When the nominative singular has one syllable, accent the ultima in the genitive and dative of all numbers. The following declension of the monosyllabic noun σάρξ, σαρκός, ἡ, "flesh" illustrates this rule.

	Singular	Plural
Nom.	σάρξ	σάρκες
Gen.	σαρκός	σαρκῶν
Dat.	σαρκί	σαρξί (ν)
Acc.	σάρκα	σάρκας
Voc.	σάρξ	σάρκες

Accusative of Extent

The accusative used without a preposition may express the extent of time or space.

ἦν ἐν τῇ ἐρήμῳ **τεσσεράκοντα ἡμέρας** πειραζόμενος (Mark 1:13); He was being tempted in the wilderness **for forty days**."

ἦλθον ἡμέρας ὁδόν (Luke 2:44); "They came a **journey** of a day."

Genitive of Time

The genitive without a preposition may express the time within which an action occurs.

προσεύχεσθε δὲ ἵνα μὴ γένηται **χειμῶνος** (Mark 13:18); "But pray that it may not be **during winter**."

οὗτος ἦλθεν πρὸς αὐτὸν **νυκτός** (John 3:2); "This man came to him **by night**."

Vocabulary

1. αἰών, αἰῶνος, ὁ — age — (aeon)
   [εἰς τὸν αἰῶνα is translated "forever," and εἰς τοὺς αἰῶνας τῶν αἰώνων is translated "forever and ever."]
2. ἄρχων, ἄρχοντος, ὁ — ruler — (ἄρχω)
3. γλῶσσα, ης, ἡ — tongue — (glossary)
4. γυνή, γυναικός, ἡ — woman — (misogynist)
5. δεύτερος, α, ον — second — (Deuteronomy)
6. θέλημα, θελήματος, τό — will — (monothelite)
7. ὄνομα, ὀνόματος, τό — name — (onomatopoeia)
8. πνεῦμα, πνεύματος, τό — spirit or wind — (pneumatic)
9. πούς, ποδός, ὁ — foot — (podium)
10. σάρξ, σαρκός, ἡ — flesh — (sarcophagus)
11. στόμα, στόματος, τό — mouth — (stomach)
12. σῶμα, σώματος, τό — body — (chromosome)
13. τρίτος, η, ον — third — (triad)
14. χαρά, ᾶς, ἡ — joy
15. χείρ, χειρός, ἡ — hand — (chirography)
16. ἀνοίγνυμι or ἀνοίγω, ἀνοίξω, ἀνέῳξα, ἀνέῳγα, ἀνέῳγμαι, ἀνεῴχθην, open
17. ἀπόλλυμι or ἀπολλύω, ἀπολέσω, ἀπώλεσα, [sec. aor. mid. ind. is ἀπωλόμην], ἀπόλωλα, --, --, destroy, [the middle voice means "die"]
18. ἅπτω, ἅψω, ἧψα, --, ἧμμαι, ἥφθην, [takes the genitive], fasten to, touch, or ignite, (haptics)
19. δείκνυμι or δεικνύω, δείξω, ἔδειξα, δέδειχα, δέδειγμαι, ἐδείχθην, show

Translation

Mark 1:39

καὶ ἦλθεν κηρύσσων (preaching) εἰς τὰς συναγωγὰς (συναγωγή, ῆς, ἡ, synagogue) αὐτῶν εἰς ὅλην τὴν Γαλιλαίαν (Γαλιλαία, ας, ἡ, Galilee) καὶ τὰ δαιμόνια ἐκβάλλων (casting out).

40 Καὶ ἔρχεται πρὸς αὐτὸν λεπρὸς (λεπρός, οῦ, ὁ, leper) παρακαλῶν (appealing to) αὐτὸν καὶ γονυπετῶν (falling on his knees) καὶ λέγων (saying) αὐτῷ ὅτι Ἐὰν (if) θέλῃς (you are willing) δύνασαί με καθαρίσαι (to cleanse). 41 καὶ σπλαγχνισθεὶς (having been moved with pity) ἐκτείνας (having stretched out) τὴν χεῖρα αὐτοῦ ἥψατο καὶ λέγει αὐτῷ, Θέλω (I will), καθαρίσθητι (be cleansed)· 42 καὶ εὐθὺς ἀπῆλθεν ἀπ' αὐτοῦ ἡ λέπρα (λέπρα, ας, ἡ, leprosy), καὶ ἐκαρίσθη (καθαρίζω, cleanse). 43 καὶ ἐμβριμησάμενος (having spoken harshly) αὐτῷ εὐθὺς ἐξέβαλεν (compound of ἐκ and βάλλω) αὐτόν, 44 καὶ λέγει αὐτῷ, Ὅρα (see) μηδενὶ (to no one) μηδὲν (anything) εἴπῃς (you say), ἀλλὰ ὕπαγε (go) σεαυτὸν δεῖξον (show) τῷ ἱερεῖ (ἱερεύς, έως, ὁ, priest) καὶ προσένεγκε (present) περὶ τοῦ καθαρισμοῦ (καθαρισμός, οῦ, ὁ, purification rites) σου ἃ προσέταξεν (compound verb of πρός and τάσσω, command) Μωϋσῆς (Μωϋσῆς, έως, ὁ, Moses) εἰς μαρτύριον (μαρτύριον, ου, τό, testimony) αὐτοῖς. 45 ὁ δὲ (ὁ δέ, he) ἐξελθὼν (having gone out) ἤρξατο κηρύσσειν (to preach) πολλὰ (frequently) καὶ διαφημίζειν (to spread) τὸν λόγον, ὥστε μηκέτι αὐτὸν δύνασθαι φανερῶς εἰς πόλιν εἰσελθεῖν (translate the eight preceding words "with the results that he was no longer able to enter publicly a city"), ἀλλ' ἔξω ἐπ' ἐρήμοις* τόποις ἦν· καὶ ἤρχοντο πρὸς αὐτὸν πάντοθεν (from all directions).

---

* In the New Testament ἔρημος is either a two ending adjective (ἔρημος, ον, see on page 146) or a feminine substantive (ἔρημος, ου, ἡ, as in Mark I: 3, 4, 12, and 13). In Classical Greek ἔρημος is either a three ending adjective (ἔρημος, η, ον) or a two ending adjective.

John 12:34

ἡμεῖς ἠκούσαμεν ἐκ τοῦ νόμου ὅτι ὁ Χριστὸς (Χριστός, οῦ, ὁ, Christ) μένει (μένω, remain) εἰς τὸν αἰῶνα.

Phil 4:20

τῷ δὲ θεῷ ... [ἐστι] ἡ δόξα εἰς τοὺς αἰῶνας τῶν αἰώνων.

Rev. 7:15

λατρεύουσιν (λατρεύω, worship) αὐτῷ ἡμέρας καὶ νυκτὸς (νύξ, νυκτός, ἡ night) ἐν τῷ ναῷ (ναός, οῦ, ὁ, temple) αὐτοῦ.

The Apology XXXII:12-13

ἡμέρας καὶ νύκτας ... βεβίωκεν (βιόω, live).

Chapter XVII

More Third Declension Nouns
Second Aorist Verbs with First Aorist Endings
Subject and Predicate Agreement

More Third Declension Nouns

The endings given in chapter XVI will suffice for the majority of third declension nouns. Nonetheless, some third declension nouns deviate from the norm. The following declensions show some of these deviations:

Singular

	ἡ	ὁ	ἡ	τό	ὁ	ὁ
Nom.	χάρις	βασιλεύς	πόλις	ἔθνος	ἀνήρ	πατήρ
Gen.	χάριτος	βασιλέως	πόλεως	ἔθνους	ἀνδρός	πατρός
Dat.	χάριτι	βασιλεῖ	πόλει	ἔθνει	ἀνδρί	πατρί
Acc.	χάριν	βασιλέα	πόλιν	ἔθνος	ἄνδρα	πατέρα
Voc.	χάρις	βασιλεῦ	πόλι	ἔθνος	ἄνερ	πάτερ

Singular

	ἡ	ὁ	ἡ	τό	ὁ	ὁ
Nom.	χάριτες	βασιλεῖς	πόλεις	ἔθνη	ἄνδρες	πατέρες
Gen.	χαρίτων	βασιλέων	πόλεων	ἐθνῶν	ἀνδρῶν	πατέρων
Dat.	χάρισι (ν)	βασιλεῦσι (ν)	πόλεσι (ν)	ἔθνεσι (ν)	ἀνδράσι (ν)	πατράσι (ν)
Acc.	χάριτας	βασιλεῖς	πόλεις	ἔθνη	ἄνδρας	πατέρας
Voc.	χάριτες	βασιλεῖς	πόλεις	ἔθνη	ἄνδρες	πατέρες

Observe these points of interest:
1. The accusative singular of χάρις is χάριν and not χάριτα.
2. Since the stem of βασιλεύς, βασιλε, ends with a vowel, there are deviations in the genitive singular, dative singular, and accusative plural.

3. The stem of πόλις is πολε; thus, it too deviates from the third declension chart in the genitive singular, dative singular, and accusative plural. The genitive singular has accent on the antepenult, even though the ultima is long. The accusative singular, like χάρις, has the "ν" ending.
4. ἔθνε, the stem of ἔθνος, also ends in a vowel. Like all neuters the nominative, accusative, and vocative of the same number have identical forms.
5. ἀνήρ and πατήρ have regular third declension endings, but in certain forms the accent moves (syncopations). Moreover, πατήρ has an "ε" in the penult of the accusative singular, nominative plural, genitive plural, and accusative plural.
6. All of these nouns serve as patterns; for instance, all feminine nouns ending in ις in the nominative singular and εως in the genitive singular are declined like πόλις, and all neuter nouns ending in ος in the nominative singular and ους in the genitive singular are declined like ἔθνος.

Second Aorist Stems with First Aorist Endings

Many verbs with second aorist stems have first aorist endings, particularly in the New Testament; that is, εἶπον becomes εἶπα (first person singular) and εἶδον (third person plural) becomes εἶδαν.

εἶπα τοῖς μαθηταῖς σου (Mark 9:18); "**I said** to your disciples."

προφῆται καὶ βασιλεῖς . . . οὐκ **εἶδαν** (Luke 10:24); "Prophets and kings . . . **did** not **see**."

Predicate and Subject Agreement

A verb agrees with its subject in number and person. Nevertheless, a nominative in the neuter plural regularly takes a singular verb.

σημεῖα δὲ . . . **παρακολουθήσει** (Mark 16:17); "But **signs . . . will follow**."

This does not mean that a neuter plural subject will not occur with a plural verb.

τὰ **πνεύματα** τὰ ἀκάθαρτα . . . **προσέπιπτον** αὐτῷ (Mark 3:11); "The unclean **spirits . . . were falling before** him."

A singular collective noun denoting persons may take a plural verb.

πᾶς ὁ **ὄχλος** πρὸς τὴν θάλασσαν ἐπὶ τῆς γῆς **ἦσαν** (Mark 4:1); "All the **crowd were** near the lake upon the ground."

There are many examples, however, where this pattern is not followed.

πᾶς ὁ **ὄχλος ἤρχετο** πρὸς αὐτόν (Mark 2:13); "All the **crowd was coming** to him."

When several subjects are connected by καί, they generally have a plural verb; however, the verb may agree with one of the subjects (usually the nearest) and be understood with the rest.

ἐξεπορεύετο πρὸς αὐτὸν πᾶσα ἡ Ἰουδαία **χώρα** καὶ οἱ Ἱεροσολυμῖται πάντες (Mark 1:5); "All the Judaean **country** and all the **Jerusalemites were going out** to him."

κατεδίωξεν αὐτὸν **Σίμων** καὶ οἱ μετ' αὐτοῦ (Mark 1:36); "**Simon** and **the men** with him **diligently searched for** him."

Vocabulary

1.	αἷμα, αἵματος, τό	blood	(hemoglobin)
2.	ἀμήν, adverb	indeed or amen	(amen)
3.	ἀνήρ, ἀνδρός, ὁ	man	(philander)
4.	ἀρχιερεύς, ἀρχιερέως, ὁ	high priest	(hierarch)
5.	βασιλεύς, βασιλέως, ὁ	king	(Basil)
6.	γραμματεύς, γραμματέως, ὁ	scribe	(grammar)
7.	δύναμις, δυνάμεως, ἡ	power	(dynamite)
8.	ἔθνος, ἔθνους, τό	nation	(ethnology)
9.	ἱερεύς, ἱερέως, ὁ	priest	(hieratic)
10.	μέρος, μέρους, τό	part	(meropia)
11.	μήτηρ, μητρός, ἡ	mother	(metropolis)
12.	ὄρος, ὄρους, τό	mountain	(orology)
13.	πατήρ, πατρός, ὁ	father	(patriarch)
14.	πίστις, πίστεως, ἡ	faith	(pistology)
15.	πόλις, πόλεως, ἡ	city	(acropolis)
16.	πῦρ, πυρός, τό	fire	(pyre)
17.	ὕδωρ, ὕδατος, τό	water	(hydrophobia)
18.	φῶς, φωτός, τό	light	(photograph)
19.	χάρις, χάριτος, ἡ	grace	(eucharis)
20.	ὡς, adverb or conjunction	about or as that	

21. ἀνίστημι, ἀναστήσω, ἀνέστησα or ἀνέστην, ἀνέστηκα, ἀνέσταμαι, ἀνεστάθην, rise or raise
22. εἶμι, [the root is "ι"; see appendix for conjugation], go (ion)

23. ζάω, ζήσω, ἔζησα, ἔζηκα, --, --, live, (ζωή) [the present indicative conjugation: ζῶ, ζῇς, ζῇ, ζῶμεν, ζῆτε, and ζῶσι]

24. ὑπάγω, ὑπάξω, ὑπήγαγον, ὑπῆχα, ὑπῆγμαι, ὑπήχθην, depart

25. ὑπάρχω, ὑπάρξω, ὑπῆρξα, --, --, --, [may be copulative], am or exist

Translation

With the beginning of this exercise a Greek New Testament and lexicon are required. The parentheses contain explanations or translations for constructions that have not been discussed.

Mark 2:1-9

1 εἰσελθὼν (having come) Καφαρναοὺμ (Capernaum) 2 πολλοὶ (many) ὥστε μηκέτι χωρεῖν (with the results that there was no longer room) μηδὲ (not even) 3 φέροντες (bearing) αἰρόμενον (being carried) τεσσάρων (four) 4 μὴ δυνάμενοι (not being able) προσενέγκαι (to bring) ἐξορύξαντες (having gouged out) 5 ἰδών (having seen) 6 τινες ("some" is the subject of ἦσαν) καθήμενοι (sitting) διαλογιζόμενοι (reasoning) 7 Τί (why) τίς (who) ἀφιέναι (to forgive) εἰ μὴ (except) εἷς (only) 8 ἐπιγνοὺς (having known) Τί (why) 9 τί (which) εὐκοπώτερον (easier) εἰπεῖν (to say) Ἔγειρε (arise) ἆρον (take up) περιπάτει (walk)

Matt 6:32

πάντα (all things) γὰρ ταῦτα τὰ ἔθνη ἐπιζητοῦσιν (ἐπιζητέω, seek).

John 1:39

ἦλθαν οὖν καὶ εἶδαν ποῦ (where) μένει.

Acts 16:3

ᾔδεισαν (past perf. act. ind. 3 pl., οἶδα) γὰρ ἅπαντες (nom. mas. pl., all) τὸν πατέρα αὐτοῦ ὅτι Ἕλλην (Ἕλλην, Ἕλληνος, ὁ, Greek) ὑπῆρχεν.

James 2:18

ἀλλ' ἐρεῖ (will say) τις, Σὺ πίστιν ἔχεις κἀγὼ (καί + ἐγώ) ἔργα ἔχω.

Chapter XVIII

The Adjectives πᾶς and ἀληθής
The Indefinite Pronoun τις
Numbers

πᾶς

The declension of the adjective πᾶς is as follows:

	Singular			Plural		
	M.	F.	N.	M.	F.	N.
Nom.	πᾶς	πᾶσα	πᾶν	πάντες	πᾶσαι	πάντα
Gen.	παντός	πάσης	παντός	πάντων	πασῶν	πάντων
Dat.	παντί	πάσῃ	παντί	πᾶσι (ν)	πάσαις	πᾶσι (ν)
Acc.	πάντα	πᾶσαν	πᾶν	πάντας	πάσας	πάντα

Observe:
1. The declension of πᾶς follows the third declension in the masculine and neuter genders, but follows the first declension in the feminine.
2. The accent is irregular.

πᾶς usually modifies a substantive in the predicate position and is translated "all."

ἀπὸ **πασῶν τῶν πόλεων** συνέδραμον (Mark 6:33); "From **all the cities** they ran."

οἶδε μὲν γὰρ οὐδεὶς τὸν θάνατον οὐδ' εἰ τυγχάνει τῷ ἀνθρώπῳ **πάντων** μέγιστον ὂν **τῶν ἀγαθῶν** (The Apology XVII:17-19): "For no one knows death if it is happening to be the greatest of **all good** to man."

When πᾶς modifies a singular substantive, it is normally translated "every."

εὐχαριστῶ τῷ θεῷ μου ἐπὶ **πάσῃ τῇ μνείᾳ** ὑμῶν (Philippians 1:3); "I thank my God at **every remembrance** of you."

πᾶσαν ὑμῖν τὴν ἀλήθειαν ἐρῶ (The Apology V:12-13); "I shall speak to you **every truth**."

When πᾶς modifies a singular collective noun, it is translated "all."

ἐξεπορεύετο πρὸς αὐτὸν **πᾶσα ἡ Ἰουδαία χώρα** καὶ οἱ Ἱεροσολυμῖται πάντες (Mark 1:5); "**All the Judaean country** and all the Jerusalemites were coming out to him."

διὰ **παντὸς τοῦ βίου** . . . τοιοῦτος φανοῦμαι (The Apology XXI:7-8); "Through **all my life** . . . I shall be found like this."

πᾶς may modify a substantive in the attributive position. In this construction it denotes the whole regarded as the sum of all its parts.

ἦσαν δὲ οἱ **πάντες ἄνδρες** ὡσεὶ δώδεκα (Acts 19:7); "And the **total number of men** was about twelve."

Πάντες ἄρα, ὡς ἔοικεν, **Ἀθηναῖοι** καλοὺς κἀγαθοὺς ποιοῦσι (The Apology XII:25-26); "Then **all Athenians** are making them excellent, as it seems."

πᾶς, like other adjectives, may be used substantivally.

πάντες ζητοῦσίν σε (Mark 1:37); "**All** are seeking you."

τουτὶ δή ἐστι **πάντων** χαλεπώτατον (The Apology XXVIII:3-4); "Now this is hardest **of all things**."

ἀληθής

The declension of the adjective ἀληθής, "true," follows the third declension.

	Singular		Plural	
	Mas. & Fem.	Neuter	Mas. & Fem.	Neuter
Nom.	ἀληθής	ἀληθές	ἀληθεῖς	ἀληθῆ
Gen.	ἀληθοῦς	ἀληθοῦς	ἀληθῶν	ἀληθῶν
Dat.	ἀληθεῖ	ἀληθεῖ	ἀληθέσι (ν)	ἀληθέσι (ν)
Acc.	ἀληθῆ	ἀληθές	ἀληθεῖς	ἀληθῆ
Voc.	ἀληθές	ἀληθές	ἀληθεῖς	ἀληθῆ

The endings for the nominative singular of both the masculine and feminine is ης but of the neuter is ες. When an adjective has these endings, it is declined like ἀληθής: ἀσθενής, ές; εὐγενής, ές; πλήρης, ές.

τις

The indefinite pronoun also declines like the third declension.

	Singular		Plural	
	Mas. & Fem.	Neuter	Mas. & Fem.	Neuter
Nom.	τις	τι	τινες	τινα
Gen.	τινος	τινος	τινων	τινων
Dat.	τινι	τινι	τισι (ν)	τισι (ν)
Acc.	τινα	τι	τινας	τινα

τις is a postpositive enclitic which is translated "someone," "something," "a certain one," "a certain thing," "anyone," or "anything." It is used either adjectivally or substantivally.

καί **τις ἀνὴρ** . . . ἐβαστάζετο (Acts 3:2); "And a **certain man** . . . was being carried."

ἔστιν **τις Σωκράτης** (The Apology II:11-12); "There is a **certain Socrates**."

ἦσαν δέ **τινες** τῶν γραμματέων ἐκεῖ καθήμενοι (Mark 2:6); "And **some** of the scribes were sitting there."

λέγω . . . εἴ **τις** περὶ τῶν τοιούτων σοφός ἐστιν (The Apology III:15-17); "I speak . . . if **anyone** is wise about such things."

Numbers

The number one is declined:

	Masculine	Feminine	Neuter
Nom.	εἷς	μία	ἕν
Gen.	ἑνός	μιᾶς	ἑνός
Dat.	ἑνί	μιᾷ	ἑνί
Acc.	ἕνα	μίαν	ἕν

The numbers three and four are declined:

	Mas. & Fem.	Neuter	Mas. & Fem.	Neuter
Nom.	τρεῖς	τρία	τέσσαρες	τέσσαρα
Gen.	τριῶν	τριῶν	τεσσάρων	τεσσάρων
Dat.	τρισί (ν)	τρισί (ν)	τέσσαρσι (ν)	τέσσαρσι (ν)
Acc.	τρεῖς	τρία	τέσσαρας	τέσσαρα

The number two, δύο, is indeclinable; however, there is a dative form, δυσί (v). With the exception of the first four numbers, all cardinal numbers below two hundred are indeclinable. Cardinal numbers above one hundred and ninety nine are declined the same as adjectives of the first and second declension. Ordinal numbers, numbers denoting order, also follow the first and second declension.

Just as other adjectives, numbers are used both adjectivally and substantivally.

> καὶ εἰ μὴ **ἕνα ἄρτον** οὐκ εἶχον (Mark 8:14); "And they were not having [food] except for **one loaf of bread**."
>
> ὃς ἂν σκανδαλίσῃ **ἕνα** τῶν μικρῶν τούτων . . . καλόν ἐστιν . . . εἰ . . . βέβληται εἰς τὴν θάλασσαν (Mark 9:42); "Whoever causes **one** of these little ones to stumble . . . it is good . . . if . . . he is thrown into the lake."

With a few exceptions, the new forms which are given in this chapter are declined according to the third declension. To be proficient in declining these new forms and the third declension, the student should periodically review the declension of πᾶς. In like manner, by reviewing the declension of ἀγαθός, the student studies the declensions of the first and second declension nouns, the definite article, demonstrative pronouns, the relative pronoun, the third person personal pronoun, the reflexive pronoun, and the reciprocal pronoun.

Vocabulary

1.	ἀληθής, ές	true	(ἀλήθεια)
2.	δέκα	ten	(decade)
3.	δύο [the dative is δυσί (v)]	two	(diarchy)
4.	εἷς, μία, ἕν	one	(henotheism)
5.	ἐννέα	nine	(enneastyle)
6.	ἑπτά	seven	(heptagon)
7.	ἕξ	six	(hexone)
8.	νύξ, νυκτός, ἡ	night	(nyctophobia)
9.	ὀκτώ	eight	(octagon)
10.	πᾶς, πᾶσα, πᾶν	all or every	(Pan-American)
11.	πέντε	five	(pentathlon)
12.	ῥῆμα, ῥήματος, τό	word	(rhetoric)
13.	συναγωγή, ῆς, ἡ	synagogue	(synagogue)
14.	τέσσαρες, α	four	(tetrapod)

15. τις, τι, indefinite pronoun someone or anyone
16. τρεῖς, τρία three (triangle)
17. εὐαγγελίζω, εὐαγγελίσω, εὐηγγέλισα, εὐηγγέλικα, εὐηγγέλισμαι, εὐηγγελίσθην, evangelize, (evangelize)
18. θεωρέω, θεωρήσω, ἐθεώρησα, --, --, --, behold, (theory)
19. πείθω, πείσω, ἔπεισα, πέποιθα, πέπεισμαι, ἐπείσθην, persuade
20. προσκυνέω, προσκυνήσω, προσεκύνησα, --, --, --, [may take the accusative but usually takes the dative], worship

Translation

Mark 2:10-17

10 εἰδῆτε (you may see) ἀφιέναι (to forgive) 11 ἔγειρε (arise) ἆρον (take up) ὕπαγε (go) 12 ἠγέρθη (he arose) ἄρας (having taken up) ὥστε ἐξίστασθαι πάντας καὶ δοξάζειν (with the results that all were amazed and were glorifying) λέγοντας (saying)

14 παράγων (going along) Λευὶν (Levi, accusative case) τὸν τοῦ Ἀλφαίου (the son of Alphaeus) καθήμενον (sitting) Ἀκολούθει (follow) ἀναστὰς (having stood up) 15 κατακεῖσθαι αὐτὸν (that he was dining) πολλοὶ (many) ἁμαρτωλοὶ (sinners) 16 ἰδόντες (having seen) Ὅτι (how) ἁμαρτωλῶν (sinners) 17 ἀκούσας (having heard) οἱ ἰσχύοντες (the men who are being strong) οἱ κακῶς ἔχοντες (the men who are having it badly) καλέσαι (to call) ἁμαρτωλούς (sinners)

Mark 10:8

ἔσονται οἱ δύο εἰς σάρκα μίαν· ὥστε οὐκέτι εἰσὶν δύο ἀλλὰ μία σάρξ.

Luke 10:9

θεραπεύετε τοὺς ἐν αὐτῇ (the antecedent of αὐτῇ is πόλις) ἀσθενεῖς.

I Cor. 10:11

ταῦτα δὲ τυπικῶς συνέβαινεν (συμβαίνω) ἐκείνοις, ἐγράφη δὲ πρὸς νουθεσίαν ἡμῶν, εἰς οὓς τὰ τέλη τῶν αἰώνων κατήντηκεν.

Chapter XIX

The Interrogative Pronoun τίς

Questions

Liquid Verbs

τίς

The interrogative pronoun τίς is declined as follows:

	Singular		Plural	
	Mas. & Fem.	Neuter	Mas. & Fem.	Neuter
Nom.	τίς	τί	τίνες	τίνα
Gen.	τίνος	τίνος	τίνων	τίνων
Dat.	τίνι	τίνι	τίσι (ν)	τίσι (ν)
Acc.	τίνα	τί	τίνας	τίνα

Observe:
1. The only difference between the forms of τις, the indefinite pronoun, and τίς, the interrogative pronoun, is the accent.
2. The accute accent of the interrogative pronoun is never changed to the grave: τίς δύναται σωθῆναι; (Mark 10:26); "Who is able to be saved?"

The interrogative τίς may modify substantives.

ἐν τίνι αὐτὴν παραβολῇ θῶμεν; (Mark 4:30); "In **what parable** shall we place it?"

τίνα αὐτοῖν ἐν νῷ ἔχεις ἐπιστάτην λαβεῖν; (The Apology IV:23-24); "**What overseer** do you have in mind to take for them?"

τίς may be a substantive.

τίς δύναται ἀφιέναι ἁμαρτίας; (Mark 2:7); "**Who** is able to forgive sins?"

τὸ σὸν τί ἐστι πρᾶγμα; (The Apology V:2); "**What** is your trouble?"

When the accusative neuter singular of τίς is used adverbially, it is translated "why."

τί ταῦτα διαλογίζεσθε; (Mark 2:8); "**Why** are you considering these things?"

τί δὴ οὖν οὐδὲν τούτων ποιήσω; (The Apology XXIII:23); "Therefore, **why** shall I not do any of these things?"

τί, however, is not always used adverbially.

τί ἐστι τοῦτο; (Mark 1:27); "**What** is this?"

τί οὖν πρέπει ἀνδρὶ πένητι; (The Apology XXVI:23-24): "Therefore, **what** is fitting for a poor man?"

The context indicates the function of τί.

Questions

Up to this point in the grammar we have had the following types of questions:

1. A question with just the question mark:
   ἦλθες ἀπολέσαι ἡμᾶς; (Mark 1:24); "Did you come to destroy us?"
2. A question introduced by a form of τίς:
   τίνα αὐτοῖν ἐν νῷ ἔχεις; (The Apology IV:23-24): "**Whom** do you have in mind for them?"
3. A question introduced by an interrogative adverb:
   πῶς δύναται Σατανᾶς Σατανᾶν ἐκβάλλειν; (Mark 3:23); "**How** is Satan able to cast out Satan?"
   τί με δεῖ ζῆν ἐν δεσμωτηρίῳ; (The Apology XXVII:19): "**Why** is it necessary that I live in a prison?"

In addition to these questions the interrogator may indicate that he expects the answer to be either yes or no. If the answer is to be yes, a form of the negative οὐ begins the question.

οὐ μέλει σοι ὅτι ἀπολλύμεθα; (Mark 4:38); "It is a concern to you that we are perishing, isn't it?"

οὐ ταῦτα λέγεις; (The Apology XIV:8-9); "You are saying these things, aren't you?"

If the answer is to be no, a form of the negative μή begins the question.

Μή τις ἤνεγκεν αὐτῷ φαγεῖν; (John 4:33); "No one has brought him [anything] to eat, have they?"

μὴ αὐτὸν οἴει φροντίσαι θανάτου καὶ κινδύνου; (The Apology XVI:33-34); "You do not think that he was concerned about death and danger, do you?"

Liquid Verbs

A liquid verb is one whose stem ends with λ, μ, ν, or ρ. Liquid and sibilant consonants (ζ, ξ, ς, and ψ) normally do not stand together; therefore, certain changes take place in the future and the first aorist systems. In the future the "ς" is dropped and an "ε" is added. There also is often a change in the verb stem; that is, ἀποστέλλω becomes ἀποστελέω and ἀποκτείνω becomes ἀποκτενέω.

    τότε **ἀποστελεῖ** τοὺς ἀγγέλους (Mark 13:27); "Then he **will send** the angels."

    ἀποκτενοῦσιν αὐτόν (Mark 9:31); "They **will kill** him."

The future active and middle indicative conjugations of μένω are:*

	Future Active Indicative		Future Middle Indicative	
	Singular	Plural	Singular	Plural
1.	μενῶ	μενοῦμεν	μενοῦμαι	μενούμεθα
2.	μενεῖς	μενεῖτε	μενῇ	μενεῖσθε
3.	μενεῖ	μενοῦσι (ν)	μενεῖται	μενοῦνται

In the first aorist system the sigma is dropped, and the stem is often changed: ἀποστέλλω becomes ἀπέστειλα yet the stem of ἀποκτείνω remains the same.

    ἄλλον **ἀπέστειλεν**, κἀκεῖνον **ἀπέκτειναν** (Mark 12:5): "He **sent** another one and they **killed** that one."

The first aorist active and middle indicative conjugations of μένω are the following:

	First Aorist Active Ind.		First Aorist Middle Ind.	
	Singular	Plural	Singular	Plural
1.	ἔμεινα	ἐμείναμεν	ἐμεινάμην	ἐμεινάμεθα
2.	ἔμεινας	ἐμείνατε	ἐμείνω	ἐμείνασθε
3.	ἔμεινε (ν)	ἔμειναν	ἐμείνατο	ἐμείναντο

Vocabulary

1. ἀσθενής, ές   weak   (neurasthenia)
2. μή, negative adverb that is generally used with non-indicative verbs
3. ὅστις, ἥτις, ὅ τι   whoever or whatever

---

* Compare these conjugations to the present active and middle indicative conjugations of the "ε" contract verb in Chapter XIV.

indefinite relative pronoun [the declension is a combination of the relative and indefinite pronoun: the genitive singulars are οὗτινος, ἧστινος, οὗτινος and the nominative plurals are οἵτινες, αἵτινες, ἅτινα]

4. τίς, τί, interrogative pronoun   who, which, or what
5. αἴρω, ἀρῶ, ἦρα, ἦρκα, ἦρμαι, ἤρθην, rasie or take up
6. ἀναβαίνω, ἀναβήσομαι, ἀνέβην, ἀναβέβηκα, --, --, go up
7. ἀποθνήσκω, ἀποθανοῦμαι [the future stem is ἀποθανε], ἀπέθανον, --, --, --, die, (θάνατος)
8. ἀποκρίνομαι, ἀποκρινοῦμαι, ἀπεκρινάμην, --, ἀποκέκριμαι, ἀπεκρίθην [deponent], [takes the dative], answer
9. ἀποκτείνω, ἀποκτενῶ, ἀπέκτεινα, --, --, ἀπεκτάνθην, kill
10. ἀποστέλλω, ἀποστελῶ, ἀπέστειλα, ἀπέσταλκα, ἀπέσταλμαι, ἀπεστάλην, send, (ἀπόστολος)
11. ἐγείρω, ἐγερῶ, ἤγειρα, --, ἐγήγερμαι, ἠγέρθην [may be deponent], raise or rise
12. ἐκβάλλω, ἐκβαλῶ, ἐξέβαλον, ἐκβέβληκα, ἐκβέβλημαι, ἐξεβλήθην, send away or throw out
13. ἔρω [obsolete], ἐρῶ, --, εἴρηκα, εἴρημαι, ἐρρήθην, say
14. θέλω [the present was originally ἐθέλω, and the imperfect is formed on the older form: ἤθελον], θελήσω, ἠθέλησα, --, --, --, will or wish, (θέλημα)
15. κρίνω, κρινῶ, ἔκρινα, κέκρικα, κέκριμαι, ἐκρίθην, judge (critic)
16. μένω, μενῶ, ἔμεινα, μεμένηκα, --, --, remain

Translation

Mark 2:18-25

18 νηστεύοντες (fasting) 19 νηστεύειν (to fast) 20 ὅταν (whenever) ἀπαρθῇ (shall be taken away) 21 εἰ δὲ μή (otherwise) χεῖρον ("more severe," predicate complement) 22 εἰ δὲ μή (otherwise)

23 αὐτὸν (translate as the subject of a noun clause: "that **he**") παραπορεύεσθαι (was going) ποιεῖν (to make) τίλλοντες (picking) 24 Ἴδε (behold) ἔξεστιν (it is lawful)

Matt 5:46

ἐὰν γὰρ ἀγαπήσητε (you love) τοὺς ἀγαπῶντας (the ones who are loving) ὑμᾶς, τίνα μισθὸν ἔχετε;

I Cor. 9:1

οὐκ εἰμὶ ἐλεύθερος; οὐκ εἰμὶ ἀπόστολος; οὐχὶ Ἰησοῦν τὸν κύριον ἡμῶν ἑώρακα; οὐ τὸ ἔργον μου ὑμεῖς ἐστε ἐν κυρίῳ;

I Cor. 1:13

μεμέρισται ὁ Χριστός; μὴ Παῦλος ἐσταυρώθη ὑπὲρ ὑμῶν, ἢ εἰς τὸ ὄνομα Παύλου ἐβαπτίσθητε;

Mark 8:36

τί γὰρ ὠφελεῖ ἄνθρωπον κερδῆσαι (to gain) τὸν κόσμον ὅλον καὶ ζημιωθῆναι (to forfeit) τὴν ψυχὴν αὐτοῦ;

Mark 14:63

τί ἔτι χρείαν ἔχομεν μαρτύρων;

Chapter XX

The Infinitive

Introduction

The infinitive is a verbal noun. Its noun qualities are seen in that it has case, gender and number; also it may be modified by the definite article. Since the infinitive is indeclinable, the context indicates its case; however, it is never used in the vocative. Its number is always singular, and its gender is always neuter.

Its verbal qualities are seen in that it has tense, may have voice, has a subject, may have an object, and may be modified by an adverb. The tense is timeless and express kind of action. The present tense denotes continuous action; the aorist is undefined action; and the perfect indicates that an action has been completed with the results remaining. The future infinitive, which is relatively rare, is sometimes used in indirect discourse.

If the subject of the infinitive is the same as the subject or object of the governing verb, the subject of the infinitive is not normally expressed. When the subject of the infinitive is expressed, it stands in the accusative case.

ποιήσω **ὑμᾶς** γενέσθαι ἁλιεῖς ἀνθρώπων (Mark 1:17); "I shall make **you** to become fishers of men."

The voice of the infinitive shows the relation of its subject to its action. When a verb is deponent in a particular tense system in the indicative mood, the infinitive will also be deponent in that tense system.

When a verb requires a particular case for an object, the infinitive of this verb requires the same case: ἀκοῦσαι **αὐτοῦ** (Luke 6:18), "to hear **him**;" πιστεῦσαι **αὐτῷ** (Matt. 21:32), "to believe **him**;" δοξάζειν τὸν θεόν (Mark 2:12), "to glorify **God**."

Except in indirect discourse, the negative for the infinitive is μή.

Form

The endings for the infinitive are εν, αι, ναι, and σθαι. These endings are suffixed to regular verbs (λύω), contract verbs (τιμάω, δηλόω, and φιλέω), liquid verbs (μένω), second aorists (ἔρχομαι), and μι verbs (εἰμι and ἵστημι) in the following manner:

Active Voice

Verb	Present	Future	Aorist	Perfect
λύω	λύειν	λύσειν	λῦσαι	λελυκέναι
τιμάω	τιμᾶν	τιμήσειν	τιμῆσαι	τετιμηκέναι
δηλόω	δηλοῦν	δηλώσειν	δηλῶσαι	δεδηλωκέναι
φιλέω	φιλεῖν	φιλήσειν	φιλῆσαι	πεφιληκέναι
μένω	μένειν	μενεῖν	μεῖναι	μεμενηκέναι
ἔρχομαι			ἐλθεῖν	ἐληλυθέναι
εἰμι	εἶναι			
ἵστημι	ἱστάναι	στήσειν	στῆσαι	
			στῆναι	

Middle and Passive Voice

Verb	Present M. & P.	Future M.	Aorist M.	Perfect M. & P.	Aorist P.*
λύω	λύεσθαι	λύσεσθαι	λύσασθαι	λελύσθαι	λυθῆναι
					λυθήσεσθαι
τιμάω	τιμᾶσθαι	τιμήσεσθαι	τιμήσασθαι	τετιμῆσθαι	τιμηθῆναι
					τιμηθήσεσθαι
δηλόω	δηλοῦσθαι	δηλώσεσθαι	δηλώσασθαι	δεδηλῶσθαι	δηλωθῆναι
					δηλωθήσεσθαι
φιλέω	φιλεῖσθαι	φιλήσεσθαι	φιλήσασθαι	πεφιλῆσθαι	φιληθῆναι
					φιληθήσεσθαι
μένω	μένεσθαι	μενεῖσθαι	μείνασθαι		
ἔρχομαι	ἔρχεσθαι	ἐλεύσεσθαι	ἐλθέσθαι		
ἵστημι	ἵστασθαι	στήσεσθαι	στήσασθαι	ἐστάσθαι	στηθῆναι
					στηθήσεσθαι

Observe:

1. The infinitival ending for the present and second aorist active of "ω" verbs and also for the future active of μι and "ω" verbs is εν. This ending, however, contracts with the variable vowel "ε" and becomes ειν: λύειν, λύσειν, and ἐλθεῖν.

2. The present active of τιμάω (τιμᾶν) does not follow the contract chart on p. 68: there is no iota subscript.

---

* The first form given is the aorist and the second is the future; however, both are built on the sixth principle part.

3. The first aorist active infinitive has accent on the penult: λῦσαι and πιστεῦσαι.

Uses

In the following illustrations the tense of the infinitives is either present or aorist. The present infinitive indicates continuous action, and the aorist indicates undefined action. This distinction, however, is often awkward to make in an English translation; therefore, in the illustrations an attempt to show the different kinds of action will not always be made. Moreover, the Greek infinitive has a much wider range of usage than the English infinitive. Consequently, it is frequently impossible to translate the Greek infinitive as an English infinitive. The objective of the translator is to convey the meaning that an author had in mind.

Like other nouns the infinitive may be used as the subject or object of a verb.

οὐκ ἔξεστίν σοι **ἔχειν** [subject] τὴν γυναῖκα τοῦ ἀδελφοῦ σου (Mark 6:18); "**To have** your brother's wife is not lawful for you."

οἱ μαθηταὶ αὐτοῦ ἤρξαντο ὁδὸν **ποιεῖν** [object] (Mark 2:23); "His disciples began **to make** a way."

τὸ γὰρ μὴ **αἰσχυνθῆναι** [subject] . . . ἔδοξεν αὐτῶν ἀναισχυντότατον **εἶναι** [object] (The Apology I:9-11); "For them not **to be ashamed** . . . seemed **to be** most shameless of them."

It also may be used as a predicate complement and as an appositive.

τὸν λόγον ἐκράτησαν πρὸς ἑαυτοὺς συζητοῦντες τί ἐστιν τὸ ἐκ νεκρῶν **ἀναστῆναι** [predicate compliment] (Mark 9:10); "They kept the saying, questioning among [to] themselves what is **to rise** from the dead."

θρησκεία . . . αὕτη ἐστίν, **ἐπισκέπτεσθαι** [appositive] ὀρφανοὺς καὶ χήρας (James 1:27); "This is religion . . . **to visit** orphans and widows."

The infinitive occasionally defines the meaning of adjectives and nouns which express ability, fitness, or kindred ideas.

οὐκ εἰμὶ ἱκανὸς . . . **λῦσαι** τὸν ἱμάντα (Mark 1:7); "I am not worthy . . . **to loose** the strap."

ἐξουσίαν ἔχει ὁ υἱὸς τοῦ ἀνθρώπου **ἀφιέναι** ἁμαρτίας (Mark 2:10); "The son of man has authority **to forgive** sins."

The absolute infinitive, one that functions as a predicate, is used to convey greetings and commands.

ταῖς δώδεκα φυλαῖς . . . **χαίρειν** (James 1:1); "To the twelve tribes . . . **greetings**."

μήτε **θαυμάζειν** μήτε **θορυβεῖν** τούτου ἕνεκα (The Apology I:29-30); "Neither **marvel** nor **make a disturbance** because of this."

The infinitive is often used to express the purpose of the action of a verb. This may be done by the simple infinitive, the articular infinitive in the genitive case, the articular infinitive with πρός, or the articular infinitive with εἰς.

οὐκ ἦλθον **καλέσαι** δικαίους ἀλλὰ ἁμαρτωλούς (Mark 2:17); "I did not come **to call** the righteous but sinners."

μέλλει γὰρ Ἡρῴδη ζητεῖν τὸ παιδίον **τοῦ ἀπολέσαι** αὐτό (Matthew 2:13); "For Herod intends to seek the child **in order that** he **may kill** him."

σκεῦος ἐκλογῆς ἐστίν μοι οὗτος **τοῦ βαστάσαι** τὸ ὄνομά μου ἐνώπιον ἐθνῶν (Acts 9:15): "This man is a chosen vessel for me **in order that** he **may bear** my name before the Gentiles."

οἱ δὲ ἀρχιερεῖς . . . ἐζήτουν κατὰ τοῦ Ἰησοῦ μαρτυρίαν **εἰς τὸ θανατῶσαι** αὐτόν (Mark 14:55); "And the chief priests . . . were seeking witness against Jesus **in order that** they **might kill** him."

οὗτος . . . ἐκάκωσεν τοὺς πατέρας . . . **εἰς τὸ μὴ ζῳογονεῖσθαι** (Acts 7:19); "This man . . . mistreated our fathers . . . **in order that** they **might** not **live**."

ἐγερθήσονται γὰρ ψευδόχριστοι . . . καὶ δώσουσιν σημεῖα . . . **πρὸς τὸ ἀποπλανᾶν** (Mark 13:22); "For false christs will arise . . . and will give signs . . . **in order that** they **may lead astray**."

πάντα δὲ τὰ ἔργα αὐτῶν ποιοῦσιν **πρὸς τὸ θεαθῆσαι** τοῖς ἀνθρώποις (Matthew 23:5); "But they do all their works **in order that** they **may be seen** by men."

ἐν τῷ with the present infinitive usually denotes contemporaneous action.

καὶ ἐγένετο **ἐν τῷ σπείρειν** (Mark 4:4); "And it happened **while** he **was sowing**."

ἰδὼν αὐτοὺς βασανιζομένους **ἐν τῷ ἐλαύειν** . . . ἔρχεται πρὸς αὐτοὺς (Mark 6:48); "Because he saw them being distressed **while** they **were rowing**, . . . he came to them."

The articular infinitive is used with several prepositions, and the vocabulary meaning of these prepositions is retained in translation.

διὰ τὸ τὴν τέχνην καλῶς **ἐξεργάζεσθαι** ἕκαστος ἠξίου . . . σοφώτατος εἶναι (The Apology VIII:9-10); "**Because** their art **was practiced** well, each one thought . . . that he was very wise."

μετὰ δὲ τὸ παραδοθῆναι τὸν Ἰωάννην ἦλθεν ὁ Ἰησοῦς (Mark 1:14); "And **after** John **was handed over**, Jesus came."

οἶδεν γὰρ ὁ πατὴρ ὑμῶν ὧν χρείαν ἔχετε **πρὸ τοῦ ὑμᾶς αἰτῆσαι** αὐτόν (Matthew 6:8); "For your father knows of what you have need **before** you **ask** him."

The infinitive with ὥστε expresses results.

ἐξῆλθεν ἔμπροσθεν πάντων, **ὥστε ἐξίστασθαι** πάντας καὶ **δοξάζειν** τὸν θεόν (Mark 2:12); "He went out before all **with the results that** all **were amazed** and **were glorifying** God."

πολλαὶ μὲν ἀπέχθειαί μοι γεγόνασι . . . **ὥστε** πολλὰς διαβολὰς ἀπ' αὐτῶν **γεγονέναι** (The Apology IX:2-5); "Many enmities have arisen against me. . . **with the results that** many prejudices **have come** from them."

The infinitive may be used as indirect discourse after certain verbs.

ἔρχονται Σαδδουκαῖοι . . . οἵτινες **λέγουσιν** ἀνάστασιν μὴ **εἶναι** (Mark 12:18); "Sadducees came . . . who **said that** there was no resurrection."

ἐὰν γράφηται . . . οὐδ' αὐτὸν **οἶμαι** τὸν κόσμον **χωρῆσαι** τὰ γραφόμενα βιβλία (John 21:25); "If it were written, . . . I do not **think that** the world itself **would hold** the books that would be written."

ὁμολογοίην . . . εἶναι ῥήτωρ (The Apology I:14-15): "**I would agree** . . . **that I am** an orator."

Vocabulary

1. δώδεκα   twelve   (Dodecanese)
2. ὀργή, ῆς, ἡ   anger   (orgy)
3. τοιοῦτος, τοιαύτη, τοιοῦτο,   such or similar
   demonstrative pronoun, [usually used without an article but stands in the attributive position if article is used].
4. χρεία, ας, ἡ   need
5. ὥστε, conjunction   so that
6. ἀναγιγνώσκω or ἀναγινώσκω, ἀναγνώσομαι, ἀνέγνων, ἀνέγνωκα, ἀνέγνωσμαι, ἀνεγνώσθην, read, (γινώσκω)
7. δεῖ, impersonal verb   "it is necessary"
   [used only in the third person; the imperfect is ἔδει]
8. ἔξεστιν, impersonal verb   "it is lawful"
   [used only in the third person]
9. καταβαίνω, καταβήσομαι, κατέβην, καταβέβηκα, --, --, go down
10. μέλλω, μελλήσω, ἐμέλλησα, --, --, --, [with an infinitive], about

11. προσκαλέω, προσκαλέσω, προσεκάλεσα, προσκέκληκα, προσκέκλημαι, προσεκλήθην, call or invite (καλέω)

12. χαίρω, χαρήσομαι, --, --, --, ἐχάρην, rejoice

Translation

Mark 2:26-3:5

26 ἐπὶ Ἀβιαθὰρ ἀρχιερέως (at the time of Abiathar the High Priest) εἰ μὴ (except) τοῖς σὺν αὐτῷ οὖσιν (the men who were with him)

3:1 ἐξηραμμένην ἔχων τὴν χεῖρα (who was having a hand withered) 2 ἵνα κατηγορήσωσιν αὐτοῦ (in order that they might bring charges against him) 3 τῷ τὴν ξηρὰν χεῖρα ἔχοντι (who was having the withered hand) Ἔγειρε (arise) 4 οἱ δὲ ἐσιώπων (they were being silent) 5 περιβλεψάμενος (having looked around at) συλλυπούμενος (being deeply grieved) Ἔκτεινον (stretch out) ἀπεκατεστάθη (ἀποκαθίστημι)

II Thes. 2:11

πέμπει αὐτοῖς ὁ θεὸς ἐνέργειαν πλάνης εἰς τὸ πιστεῦσαι αὐτοὺς τῷ ψεύδει.

John 1:48

πρὸ τοῦ σε Φίλιππον φωνῆσαι ... εἶδόν σε.

Mark 5:4

διὰ τὸ αὐτὸν πολλάκις πέδαις καὶ ἁλύσεσιν δεδέσθαι (perf. pass. inf. δέω) καὶ διεσπάσθαι (perf. pass. inf. διασπάω) ... καὶ οὐδεὶς ἴσχυεν αὐτὸν δαμάσαι.

Luke 1:8

ἐγένετο δὲ ἐν τῷ ἱερατεύειν αὐτὸν ἐν τῇ τάξει τῆς ἐφημερίας αὐτοῦ.

Luke 19:15

εἶπεν φωνηθῆναι αὐτῷ τοὺς δούλους τούτους οἷς δεδώκει τὸ ἀργύριον.

Matt 12:22

ἐθεράπευσεν αὐτόν, ὥστε τὸν κωφὸν λαλεῖν καὶ βλέπειν.

II Cor. 3:13

ἐτίθει κάλυμμα ἐπὶ τὸ πρόσωπον αὐτοῦ πρὸς τὸ μὴ ἀτενίσαι τοὺς υἱούς.

Chapter XXI

The Present and Future Active Participles
The Attributive and Substantival Uses of the Participle

Introduction

The participle* is a verbal adjective. Its verbal qualities are that it may have tense, voice, an object, and an adverb modifier. The tense of a participle is timeless and expresses kind of action. Its voice indicates the relation of its action to the word that it modifies; that is, with the active participle the modified word does the action; with the middle participle the modified word does the action with special interest to itself; with the passive participle the modified word receives the action. The object of the participle is in the same case as if it were the object of the verb form of the participle. Normally, μή is used to negate the participle.** Its adjectival qualities are that it has case, gender, number, and may stand in either the attributive or predicate position (Chapter IV).

The Present and Future Active Participle

The declensions of the present active participles of λύω and φιλέω are as follows:

Singular

	Mas.	Fem.	Neuter	Mas.	Fem.	Neuter
Nom. & Voc.	λύων	λύουσα	λῦον	φιλῶν	φιλοῦσα	φιλοῦν
Gen.	λύοντος	λυούσης	λύοντος	φιλοῦντος	φιλούσης	φιλοῦντος
Dat.	λύοντι	λυούσῃ	λύοντι	φιλοῦντι	φιλούσῃ	φιλοῦντι
Acc.	λύοντα	λύουσαν	λῦον	φιλοῦντα	φιλοῦσαν	φιλοῦν

---

* Because of the importance of the participle and because of the difficulty the beginning student usually has in mastering it, these next few chapters are short. The brevity of the chapters, however, does not indicate that the student may spend less time studying. An intense effort in studying the participle is most necessary in understanding and using the Greek language.

** When the participle refers to an actual fact, its negative is usually οὐ: Ἔστιν δὲ πίστις . . . ἔλεγχος οὐ βλεπομένων (Hebrews 11:1); "Now faith is . . . certainty of things which are not being seen." μή is used for conditions or general statements.

Plural

	Mas.	Fem.	Neuter	Mas.	Fem.	Neuter
Nom. & Voc.	λύοντες	λύουσαι	λύοντα	φιλοῦντες	φιλοῦσαι	φιλοῦντα
Gen.	λυόντων	λυουσῶν	λυόντων	φιλούντων	φιλουσῶν	φιλούντων
Dat.	λύουσι(ν)	λυούσαις	λύουσι(ν)	φιλοῦσι(ν)	φιλούσαις	φιλοῦσι(ν)
Acc.	λύοντας	λυούσας	λύοντα	φιλοῦντας	φιλούσας	φιλοῦντα

Observe:
1. The present participle follows the third declension in the masculine and neuter genders and the first declension in the feminine gender.
2. The rules of contraction for verbs (Chapter XIII) apply for contract participles.

The declension of the participle of εἰμι is:

	Singular			Plural		
	Mas.	Fem.	Neuter	Mas.	Fem.	Neuter
Nom. & Voc.	ὤν	οὖσα	ὄν	ὄντες	οὖσαι	ὄντα
Gen.	ὄντος	οὔσης	ὄντος	ὄντων	οὐσῶν	ὄντων
Dat.	ὄντι	οὔσῃ	ὄντι	οὖσι(ν)	οὔσαις	οὖσι(ν)
Acc.	ὄντα	οὖσαν	ὄν	ὄντας	οὔσας	ὄντα

The declensions of the present active participles of δίδωμι and ἵστημι are as follows:

Singular

	Mas.	Fem.	Neuter	Mas.	Fem.	Neuter
Nom. & Voc.	διδούς	διδοῦσα	διδόν	ἱστάς	ἱστᾶσα	ἱστάν
Gen.	διδόντος	διδούσης	διδόντος	ἱστάντος	ἱστάσης	ἱστάντος
Dat.	διδόντι	διδούσῃ	διδόντι	ἱστάντι	ἱστάσῃ	ἱστάντι
Acc.	διδόντα	δοδοῦσαν	διδόν	ἱστάντα	ἱστᾶσαν	ἱστάν

Plural

	Mas.	Fem.	Neuter	Mas.	Fem.	Neuter
Nom. & Voc.	διδόντες	διδοῦσαι	διδόντα	ἱστάντες	ἱστᾶσαι	ἱστάντα
Gen.	διδόντων	διδουσῶν	διδόντων	ἱστάντων	ἱστασῶν	ἱστάντων
Dat.	διδοῦσι(ν)	διδούσαις	διδοῦσι(ν)	ἱστᾶσι(ν)	ἱστάσαις	ἱστᾶσι(ν)
Acc.	διδόντας	διδούσας	διδόντα	ἱστάντας	ἱστάσας	ἱστάντα

Except for being built on the second of the principal parts, the future active declension of the participle is the same as the declension of the present active.

	Singular			Plural		
	Mas.	Fem.	Neuter	Mas.	Fem.	Neuter
Nom. & Voc.	λύσων	λύσουσα	λῦσον	λύσοντες	λύσουσαι	λύσοντα
Gen.	λύσοντος	λυσούσης	λύσοντος	λυσόντων	λυσουσῶν	λυσόντων
Dat.	λύσοντι	λυσούσῃ	λύσοντι	λύσουσι (ν)	λυσούσαις	λύσουσι (ν)
Acc.	λύσοντα	λύσουσαν	λῦσον	λύσοντας	λυσούσας	λύσοντα

The Attributive and Substantival Participles

In the attributive position the participle gives an attribute of the modified substantive; thus ὁ λύων ἄνθρωπος is "the liberating man." However, the translator normally uses a relative clause to translate this construction. The need for this is particularly seen when the participle has an object: ὁ λύων δούλους ἄνθρωπος, "the man who is liberating slaves" not "the liberating slaves man." There is one small difficulty in using the relative clause; that is, the Greek participle is timeless and the verb of the relative clause which is used to translate the participle has time. This difficulty is overcome by letting the context supply the time. Study these examples:

λέγει [historical present] τῷ ἀνθρώπῳ τῷ τὴν ξηρὰν χεῖρα ἔχοντι (Mark 3:3); "He spoke **to the man who was having** the withered hand."

εὐλογημένη ἡ ἐρχομένη [present deponent] βασιλεία (Mark 11:10); "Blessed is **the kingdom which is coming.**"

πόθεν οὖν ἔχεις τὸ ὕδωρ τὸ ζῶν; (John 4:11), "Therefore, where do you have **the water which is living?**"

οὗτος ὁ Ἰησοῦς ὁ ἀναλημφθεὶς [aorist passive] ἀφ' ὑμῶν εἰς τὸν οὐρανὸν οὕτως ἐλεύσεται (Acts 1:11); "This **Jesus who was taken up** from you into heaven thus will come."

When there are no articles, the context must indicate whether the participle is in the attributive or predicate position.

γυνὴ οὖσα ἐν ῥύσει αἵματος . . . ἥψατο τοῦ ἱματίου αὐτοῦ (Mark 5:25-27); "**A woman who was** in a flow of blood . . . touched his garment."

The attributive participle, like other adjectives, may modify an understood substantive. The substantival participle is usually translated by using a relative clause.

[ἐστι] φωνὴ **βοῶντος** ἐν τῇ ἐρήμῳ (Mark 1:3); "[He is] a voice **of one who is crying** in the wilderness."

ἔδωκεν καὶ **τοῖς σὺν αὐτῷ οὖσιν** (Mark 2:26); "He also gave **to those who were** with him."

ἐξῆλθεν ὁ **σπείρων** σπεῖραι (Mark 4:3); "**The man who was sowing** went out to sow."

ἀκούσεσθε εἰκῇ **λεγόμενα** [present passive] τοῖς ἐπιτυχοῦσιν [second aorist active attributive participle] ὀνόμασιν (The Apology I:20-21); "You will hear **things which are being spoken** at random in the words which are chanced upon."

Vocabulary

1. ἄρα, conjunction — then
2. δεξιός, ά, όν — right [opposite of left] (dexterous)
3. διό, conjuction — wherefore
4. ἐλπίς, ἐλπίδος, ἡ — hope
5. ἐπαγγελία, ας, ἡ — promise
6. ἔσχατος, η, ον — last (eschatology)
7. κακός, ή, όν — bad (cacophony)
8. λίθος, ου, ὁ — stone (monolith)
9. μακάριος, α, ον — blessed
10. μᾶλλον, comp. adverb — more or rather
11. μόνος, η, ον — only or alone (monologue)
12. οὐδείς, οὐδεμία, οὐδέν — no one (εἷς)
13. παιδίον, ου, τό — child or infant (encyclopaedia)
14. πλῆθος, πλήθους, τό — crowd or multitude (plethora)
15. σοφία, ας, ἡ — wisdom (philosophy)
16. τε, conjunction — and [postpositive and enclitic, weaker in force than καί]
17. χρόνος, ου, ὁ — time (chronology)
18. ἀπαγγέλλω, ἀπαγγελῶ, ἀπήγγειλα, ἀπήγγελκα, ἀπήγγελμαι, ἀπηγγέλθην, report, (ἄγγελος)
19. ἐπιτιμάω, ἐπιτιμήσω, ἐπετίμησα, ἐπιτετίμηκα, ἐπιτετίμημαι, ἐπετιμήθην, command or rebuke, (timocracy)
20. θεραπεύω, θεραπεύσω, ἐθεράπευσα, τεθεράπευκα, τεθεράπευμαι, ἐθεραπεύθην, heal, (therapeutics)

Translation

Mark 3:6-15

6 ἐξελθόντες (having gone out) ἀπολέσωσιν (they might kill)

7 πολὺ (great) 8 ἀκούοντες (hearing) 9 προσκαρτερῇ (might be ready) μὴ θλίβωσιν (they might not crush) 10 πολλοὺς (many) ἅψωνται (they might touch) μάστιγας (μάστιξ) 11 λέγοντες (saying) 12 πολλὰ (much) ἵνα μὴ (lest) ποιήσωσιν (they make)

14 ὦσιν (they might be) ἀποστέλλῃ (he might send)

John 6:50

οὗτός ἐστιν ὁ ἄρτος ὁ ἐκ τοῦ οὐρανοῦ καταβαίνων.

Matt. 5:28

ἐγὼ δὲ λέγω ὑμῖν ὅτι πᾶς ὁ βλέπων γυναῖκα πρὸς τὸ ἐπιθυμῆσαι αὐτὴν ἤδη ἐμοίχευσεν αὐτὴν ἐν τῇ καρδίᾳ αὐτοῦ.

Acts 2:7

οὐχ ἰδοὺ ἅπαντες οὗτοί εἰσιν οἱ λαλοῦντες Γαλιλαῖοι;

Rom 12:3

λέγω γὰρ διὰ τῆς χάριτος τῆς δοθείσης (δίδωμι part. 1st aor. pass. gen. fem. s.) μοι παντὶ τῷ ὄντι ἐν ὑμῖν μὴ ὑπερφρονεῖν πάρ' ὃ δεῖ φρονεῖν, ἀλλὰ φρονεῖν εἰς τὸ σωφρονεῖν, ἑκάστῳ ὡς ὁ θεὸς ἐμέρισεν μέτρον πίστεως.

Chapter XXII

Aorist and Perfect Active Participles
Circumstantial Participles of Time and Cause

Aorist and Perfect Active Participles

The declension of the first aorist active participle of the regular verb λύω and the liquid verb μένω are as follows:

Singular

	Mas.	Fem.	Neuter	Mas.	Fem.	Neuter
N. &. V.	λύσας	λύσασα	λῦσαν	μείνας	μείνασα	μεῖναν
Gen.	λύσαντος	λυσάσης	λύσαντος	μείναντος	μεινάσης	μείναντος
Dat.	λύσαντι	λυσάσῃ	λύσαντι	μείναντι	μεινάσῃ	μείναντι
Acc.	λύσαντα	λύσασαν	λῦσαν	μείναντα	μείνασαν	μεῖναν

Plural

	Mas.	Fem.	Neuter	Mas.	Fem.	Neuter
N. &. V.	λύσαντες	λύσασαι	λύσαντα	μείναντες	μείνασαι	μείναντα
Gen.	λυσάντων	λυσασῶν	λυσάντων	μεινάντων	μεινασῶν	μεινάντων
Dat.	λύσασι (ν)	λυσάσαις	λύσασι (ν)	μείνασι (ν)	μεινάσαις	μείνασι (ν)
Acc.	λύσαντας	λυσάσας	λύσαντα	μείναντας	μεινάσας	μείναντα

The declensions of the second aorist active participle of δίδωμι and ἵστημι are as follows:

Singular

	Mas.	Fem.	Neuter	Mas.	Fem.	Neuter
N. &. V.	δούς	δοῦσα	δόν	στάς	στᾶσα	στάν
Gen.	δόντος	δούσης	δόντος	στάντος	στάσης	στάντος
Dat.	δόντι	δούσῃ	δόντι	στάντι	στάσῃ	στάντι
Acc.	δόντα	δοῦσαν	δόν	στάντα	στᾶσαν	στάν

Plural

	Mas.	Fem.	Neuter	Mas.	Fem.	Neuter
N. & V.	δόντες	δοῦσαι	δόντα	στάντες	στᾶσαι	στάντα
Gen.	δόντων	δουσῶν	δόντων	στάντων	στασῶν	στάντων
Dat.	δοῦσι (ν)	δούσαις	δοῦσι (ν)	στᾶσι (ν)	στάσαις	στᾶσι (ν)
Acc.	δόντας	δούσας	δόντα	στάντας	στάσας	στάντα

The declension of the second aorist active participle of ἔρχομαι is:

Singular

	Mas.	Fem.	Neuter	Mas.	Fem.	Neuter
N. & V.	ἐλθών	ἐλθοῦσα	ἐλθόν	ἐλθόντες	ἐλθοῦσαι	ἐλθόντα
Gen.	ἐλθόντος	ἐλθούσης	ἐλθόντος	ἐλθόντων	ἐλθουσῶν	ἐλθόντων
Dat.	ἐλθόντι	ἐλθούσῃ	ἐλθόντι	ἐλθοῦσι (ν)	ἐλθούσαις	ἐλθοῦσι (ν)
Acc.	ἐλθόντα	ἐλθοῦσαν	ἐλθόν	ἐλθόντας	ἐλθούσας	ἐλθόντα

The declension of the perfect active participle of λύω is:

Singular   Plural

	Mas.	Fem.	Neuter	Mas.	Fem.	Neuter
N. & V.	λελυκώς	λελυκυῖα	λελυκός	λελυκότες	λελυκυῖαι	λελυκότα
Gen.	λελυκότος	λελυκυίας	λελυκότος	λελυκότων	λελυκυιῶν	λελυκότων
Dat.	λελυκότι	λελυκυίᾳ	λελυκότι	λελυκόσι (ν)	λελυκυίαις	λελυκόσι (ν)
Acc.	λελυκότα	λελυκυῖαν	λελυκός	λελυκότας	λελυκυίας	λελυκότα

Circumstantial Participles of Time and Cause

The circumstantial participle modifies a substantive in the predicate position: ἡ δὲ πενθερά ... πυρέσσουσα (Mark 1:30). When the participle modifies the subject pronoun expressed within the verb, it is normally considered in the predicate position: παράγων ... εἶδεν Σίμωνα (Mark 1:6).

The circumstantial participle sets forth some circumstance under which an action, usually the main action, takes place. Thus, this participle implies various relations of itself to the verb. These various relations are indicated by the context. Many circumstances may be implied, but it will suffice for this chapter to consider only two: cause and time.

Cause

The circumstantial participle may tell why the action of the governing verb is being done.

δὴ καὶ **πιστεύων** Μέλητός με ἐγράψατο τὴν γραφὴν ταύτην (The Apology III:3-4); "And apparently **because he was believing** [it], Meletos wrote this charge against me."

ἐπιγνοὺς ὁ Ἰησοῦς τῷ πνεύματι αὐτοῦ ὅτι οὕτως διαλογίζονται . . . λέγει αὐτοῖς (Mark 2:8); "**Because he knew** in his spirit that they were reasoning like this . . ., Jesus spoke to them."

ἡ δὲ πενθερὰ Σίμωνος κατέκειτο **πυρέσσουσα** (Mark 1:30); "**Because of suffering with fever**, the mother-in-law of Simon was lying down."

A circumstantial participle may be translated either as a participial phrase or an adverbial clause. When a clause is used, the subject of the clause is the substantive that the participle modifies; however, a pronoun is usually used in the adverbial clause rather than repeating the substantive. Thus, Mark 1:30 may also be translated:

"**Because she was suffering with fever**, the mother-in-law of Simon was lying down."

Time

The circumstantial participle may express the time relation between itself and the governing verb. If this participle has present tense, its action takes place at the same time that the action of the verb does.

ἡ μήτηρ αὐτοῦ καὶ οἱ ἀδελφοὶ αὐτοῦ καὶ ἔξω **στήκοντες** ἀπέστειλαν πρὸς αὐτόν (Mark 3:31); "**While standing** outside, his mother and brothers sent to him."

καὶ **παράγων** παρὰ τὴν θάλασσαν τῆς Γαλιλαίας εἶδεν Σίμωνα (Mark 1:16); "And **while passing along** the sea of Galilee, he saw Simon."

The governing verb in this sentence, εἶδεν, is second aorist; but if it were present or future, the time relation would be the same.

καὶ **παράγων** παρὰ τὴν θάλασσαν τῆς Γαλιλαίας βλέπει Σίμωνα, "And **while passing along** the sea of Galilee, he **sees** Simon."

καὶ **παράγων** παρὰ τὴν θάλασσαν τῆς Γαλιλαίας ὄψεται Σίμωνα, "And **while passing along** the sea of Galilee, he **will see** Simon."

When the aorist participle is used to express time relation, it indicates that the action of the participle takes place before the action of the verb.

εὐθὺς **ἀφέντες** τὰ δίκτυα ἠκολούθησαν αὐτῷ (Mark 1:18); "Immediately **after having left** the nets, they followed him."

καὶ **σπαράξαν** αὐτὸν τὸ πνεῦμα τὸ ἀκάθαρτον καὶ **φωνῆσαν** φωνῇ μεγάλῃ ἐξῆλθεν ἐξ αὐτοῦ (Mark 1:26); "**After** it **convulsed** him and **cried** with a great voice, the unclean spirit came out of him."

ἄρας οὖν τὰ μέλη τοῦ Χριστοῦ ποιήσω πόρνης μέλη; (1 Corinthians 6:15); "Then **after I take** the members of Christ, shall I make [them] members of a prostitute?"

The article followed by δέ, μέν, or μὲν οὖν may stand in place of a substantive that has been previously mentioned. The article is translated as a personal pronoun.

ὁ δὲ ἐξελθὼν ἤρξατο κηρύσσειν πολλά (Mark 1:45); "And **he**, after having gone out, began to preach much."

This use creates an occasional ambiguity when the participle is involved. The participle στυγνάσας in Mark 10:22 could be either substantival or circumstantial.

ὁ δὲ στυγνάσας ἐπὶ τῷ λόγῳ ἀπῆλθεν λυπούμενος, (substantival) "And **the man who was shocked** at the word departed grieving," or (circumstantial of cause) "And **because of having been shocked** at the word, he departed grieving."

Vocabulary

1. ἔμπροσθεν, adverb followed by the gen. — in front of
2. ἐπεί, adverb — since or when
3. ἔτος, ἔτους, τό — year
4. θυσία, ας, ἡ — sacrifice
5. ἰσχυρός, ά, όν — strong
6. κρίσις, κρίσεως, ἡ — judgment (crisis)
7. μικρός, ά, όν — small (microscope)
8. οὐκέτι, adverb — no longer
   [μηκέτι is used with non-indicative verbs]
9. ποῦ, interrogative adverb — where
10. σωτηρία, ας, ἡ — salvation (soteriology)
11. τέλος, τέλους, τό — end (teleology)
12. τυφλός, ή, όν — blind (typhlosis)
13. φόβος, ου, ὁ — fear (phobia)

14. φυλακή, ῆς, ἡ   prison or guard   (phylactic)
15. καθίζω, καθίσω, ἐκάθισα, κεκάθικα, --, --, sit or set, (cathedral)
16. κρατέω, κρατήσω, ἐκράτησα, κεκράτηκα, κεκράτημαι, ἐκρατήθην, grasp, (plutocrat)
17. παραλαμβάνω, παραλήμψομαι, παρέλαβον, παρείληφα, παρείλημμαι, παρελήμφθην, receive, (λαμβάνω)
18. προσφέρω, προσοίσω, προσήνεγκα or προσήνεγκον, προσενήνοχα, προσενήνεγμαι, προσηνέχθην, offer, (φέρω)
19. σπείρω, σπερῶ, ἔσπειρα, --, ἔσπαρμαι, ἐσπάρην, sow, (spore)
20. φανερόω, φανερώσω, ἐφανέρωσα, πεφανέρωκα, πεφανέρωμαι, ἐφανερώθην, show, (cellophane)

Translation

Mark 3:16-26

17 τὸν τοῦ Ζεβεδαίου (the son of Zebedee) βοανηργές (Boanerges) 18 τὸν τοῦ Ἀλφαίου (the son of Alphaeus) 23 προσκαλεσάμενος (having called) 24 μερισθῇ (is divided) 25 μερισθῇ (is divided)

Mark 5:27

ἀκούσασα περὶ τοῦ Ἰησοῦ, ἐλθοῦσα ἐν τῷ ὄχλῳ ὄπισθεν ἥψατο τοῦ ἱματίου αὐτοῦ.

Acts 3:2

καὶ τις ἀνὴρ χωλὸς ἐκ μητρὸς αὐτοῦ ὑπάρχων ἐβαστάζετο, ὃν ἐτίθουν καθ' ἡμέραν πρὸς τὴν θύραν τοῦ ἱεροῦ τὴν λεγομένην (part. pres. pass. acc. fem. s.) Ὡραίαν τοῦ αἰτεῖν ἐλεημοσύνην παρὰ τῶν εἰσπορευομένων (part. pres. dep. gen. mas. pl.) εἰς τὸ ἱερόν.

Acts 5:4

οὐχὶ μένον σοὶ ἔμενεν καὶ πραθὲν (πιπράσκω part. 1st aor. pass. nom. n. s.) ἐν τῇ σῇ ἐξουσίᾳ ὑπῆρχεν;

Chapter XXIII

Middle Voice of the Participle
More Circumstantial Participles
Genitive Absolute

Middle Voice of the Participle

The declension of the present middle participle of λύω is as follows:

	Singular		
	Mas.	Fem.	Neuter
N. & V.	λυόμενος	λυομένη	λυόμενον
Gen.	λυομένου	λυομένης	λυομένου
Dat.	λυομένῳ	λυομένῃ	λυομένῳ
Acc.	λυόμενον	λυομένην	λυόμενον

	Plural		
	Mas.	Fem.	Neuter
N. & V.	λυόμενοι	λυόμεναι	λυόμενα
Gen.	λυομένων	λυομένων	λυομένων
Dat.	λυομένοις	λυομέναις	λυομένοις
Acc.	λυομένους	λυομένας	λυόμενα

The future, aorist, and perfect tenses also use "μεν" as a sign for the middle voice and are declined like the first and second declensions. Observe the following nominative singular forms:

διδόμενος, η, ον — present middle of δίδωμι
ἱστάμενος, η, ον — present middle of ἵστημι
λυσόμενος, η, ον — future middle of λύω
λυσάμενος, η, ον — first aorist middle of λύω
λαβόμενος, η, ον — second aorist middle of λαμβάνω
λελυμένος, η, ον — perfect middle of λύω

The significance of the voice of a participle is the same as that of a verb. When a participle has middle voice, the modified word does the action of the participle but with special interest to itself. The context and the lexical meaning of the participle indicate what this interest is. If an indicative verb is deponent, the corresponding tense of the participle will also be deponent: the present participle of ἔρχομαι is ἐρχόμενος, η, ον.

More Circumstantial Participles

The circumstantial participle, as pointed out in the preceding chapter, may express temporal or causal relations. In addition, it may express manner, means, identical action, condition, concession, or attendant circumstance. The context (not the participle) governs the adverbial relation that the translation should reflect. Moreover, in certain contexts, more than one relation may be plausible; that is, **ἐπιγνοὺς** ὁ Ἰησοῦς τῷ πνεύματι αὐτοῦ ὅτι οὕτως διαλογίζονται ἐν ἑαυτοῖς λέγει αὐτοῖς (Mark 2:8); could be translated, "**Because** he knew in his spirit that they were reasoning thus among themselves, Jesus spoke to them," or it could be, "**After** he knew in his spirit that they were reasoning thus among themselves, Jesus spoke to them." The translator's responsibility is to express the thought which the author was conveying.

The circumstantial participle of manner describes the manner in which the action of the verb is carried out.

ἦλθεν ὁ Ἰησοῦς εἰς τὴν Γαλιλαίαν **κηρύσσων** τὸ εὐαγγέλιον (Mark 1:14); "Jesus came into Galilee **preaching** the gospel."

τούτους πείθουσι . . . **διδόντας** καὶ χάριν (The Apology IV:11-13); "They are persuading these men . . . and **giving** thanks."

The circumstantial participle of means tells how the action of the verb is carried out. Its phrase or clause may be introduced with the word "by."

ἐπετίμησεν αὐτῷ ὁ Ἰησοῦς **λέγων**, Φιμώθητι (Mark 1:25); "Jesus rebuked him **by saying**, 'Be silent.'"

ὑμῶν τοὺς πολλοὺς ἐκ παίδων **παραλαμβάνοντες** ἔπειθον (The Apology II:9-10); "**By taking** the many of you from childhood, they were persuading [you]."

Study the following sentence, paying particular attention to **scratching** and **walking**:

Scratching his head, the boy went to town by **walking**.

Scratching describes what the boy is doing as he goes to town (circumstantial of manner). **Walking** tells the means that the boy used to go the town (circumstantial of means).

The circumstantial participle may be the **the identical action** expressed by the verb.

ἀποκριθεὶς αὐτοῖς λέγει [historical present] (Mark 3:33);
"**Answering** he spoke to them."
εἶπαν αὐτῷ **λέγοντες** (Mark 8:28); "They spoke to him **saying**."

In each of the above passages, note that the action of the participle and the verb not only takes place at the same time, but it is the same action.

The circumstantial participle of concession tells that in spite of a difficulty indicated by this participle, the main action of the verb is carried out. "Although" usually introduces this clause or phrase.

εἰ οὖν ὑμεῖς πονηροὶ **ὄντες** οἴδατε δόματα ἀγαθὰ διδόναι τοῖς τέκνοις ὑμῶν, πόσῳ μᾶλλον ὁ πατὴρ ὑμῶν ὁ ἐν τοῖς οὐρανοῖς δώσει ἀγαθὰ τοῖς αἰτοῦσιν αὐτόν (Matt 7:11); "Therefore if you yourselves, **although being** evil, know to give good gifts to your children, how much more will your father in heaven give good gifts to the ones who are asking him."

οὓς ἐγὼ μᾶλλον φοβοῦμαι ἢ τοὺς ἀμφὶ Ἄνυτον, καίπερ **ὄντας** καὶ τούτους δεινούς (The Apology II:7-8); "Whom I fear more than the men around Anytus, **although** these also **are** fearful."

The circumstantial participle of condition serves as the protasis of a conditional sentence.

πῶς ἡμεῖς ἐκφευξόμεθα τηλικαύτης **ἀμελήσαντες** σωτηρίας (Hebrews 2:3); "**If we neglect** so great a salvation, how shall we ourselves escape?"

The circumstantial participle of attendant circumstance does not present in a distinct way any of the above adverbial relations, but does express an additional thought or fact.

τότε ὑπέστρεψαν εἰς Ἰερουσαλὴμ ἀπὸ ὄρους τοῦ καλουμένου Ἐλαιῶνος, ὅ ἐστιν ἐγγὺς Ἰερουσαλὴμ σαββάτου **ἔχον** ὁδόν (Acts 1:12); "Then they returned unto Jerusalem from the mountain which is called Olivet, which is near Jerusalem, **having** a journey of a Sabbath."

Genitive Absolute

A genitive absolute construction consists both of a genitive substantive (this substantive is the genitive absolute) which is not directly dependent on the other parts of the sentence and a circumstantial participle that modifies the genitive substantive. Study the following example:

ὀψίας δὲ γενομένης, ὅτε ἔδυ ὁ ἥλιος, ἔφερον πρὸς αὐτὸν πάντας τοὺς κακῶς ἔχοντας καὶ τοὺς δαιμονιζομένους (Mark 1:32); "And **after evening had come**, when the sun had set, they were bringing to him all the sick (the ones who were having it badly) and the ones where were being demon possessed."

Since ὀψίας is neither the subject, object, nor indirect object, nor does it immediately go with them, it is an absolute. The circumstantial participle in a genitive absolute construction may express most of the adverbial relations that have been discussed. The following are more examples of genitive absolute constructions:

ἐμβαίνοντος αὐτοῦ εἰς τὸ πλοῖον παρεκάλει αὐτὸν ὁ δαιμονισθεὶς ἵνα μετ' αὐτοῦ ᾖ (Mark 5:18); "**While he was embarking** into the boat, the man who had been demon possessed was beseeching him in order that he might be with him."

ἔπειτά εἰσιν οὗτοι οἱ κατήγοροι πολλοί . . . ἐρήμην κατηγοροῦντες, ἀπολογουμένου οὐδενός (The Apology II:17-22); "Next these accusers are many . . . defaulting the charges, **because no one was defending**."

καὶ διαπεράσαντος τοῦ Ἰησοῦ πάλιν εἰς τὸ πέραν συνήχθη ὄχλος πολὺς (Mark 5:21); "And **after Jesus crossed** again unto the other side, a great crowd gathered."

Vocabulary

1. ἀνάστασις, εως, ἡ	resurrection	(apostasy)
2. ἄξιος, α, ον	worthy	(axiom)
3. ἅπας, ἅπασα, ἅπαν [intensified form of πᾶς]	all	
4. γενεά, ᾶς, ἡ	generation	(genealogy)
5. ἐπιθυμία, ας, ἡ	eager desire or lust	
6. θηρίον, ου, τό	wild beast	(therimorphic)
7. θλῖψις, εως, ἡ	tribulation	
8. θυγάτηρ, θυγατρός, ἡ	daughter	

9. θύρα, ας, ἡ — door (thyroid)
10. ἱκανός, ή, όν — able or sufficient
11. ναός, οῦ, ὁ — temple or inner part of a temple (naos)
12. οἰκία, ας, ἡ — house (dioecious)
13. οἵμοιος, α, ον — like (homonym)
14. σήμερον, adverb — today
15. σπέρμα, σπέρματος, τό — seed (sperm)
16. ἁμαρατάνω, ἁμαρτήσω, ἡμάρτησα, or ἥμαρτον, ἡμάρτηκα, ἡμάρτημαι, ἡμαρτήθην, sin, (ἁμαρτία)
17. δέω, δήσω, ἔδησα, δέδεκα, δέδεμαι, ἐδέθην, tie, (diadem)
18. διώκω, διώξω, ἐδίωξα, δεδίωκα, δεδίωγμαι, ἐδιώχθην, persecute or pursue
19. ἐγγίζω, ἐγγίσω, ἤγγισα, ἤγγικα, --, --, draw near
20. ἐπιγιγνώσκω or ἐπιγινώσκω, ἐπιγνώσομαι, ἐπέγνων, ἐπέγνωκα, ἐπέγνωσομαι, ἐπεγνώσθην, understand or know well
21. εὐλογέω, εὐλογήσω, εὐλόγησα, εὐλόγηκα, εὐλόγημαι, εὐλογήθην, bless, (euology)

Translation

Mark 3:27-35

27 ἐὰν μὴ (unless) πρῶτον (adverb, "first") δήσῃ (he tie)   28 ὅσα ἐὰν βλασφημήσωσιν (as many as they may blaspheme)   29 ὃς δ' ἂν βλασφημήσῃ (but whoever blasphemes)

ὃς γὰρ ἂν ποιήσῃ (for whoever does)

The Apology III:3,4

τί δὴ λέγοντες διέβαλλον (διαβάλλω, create prejudice) οἱ διαβάλλοντες;

Acts 4:37

ὑπάρχοντος αὐτῷ ἀγροῦ πωλήσας ἤνεγκεν τὸ χρῆμα καὶ ἔθηκεν παρὰ τοὺς πόδας τῶν ἀποστόλων.

Gal. 6:9

τὸ δὲ καλὸν ποιοῦντες μὴ ἐγκακῶμεν (let us tire), καιρῷ γὰρ ἰδίῳ θερίσομεν μὴ ἐκλυόμενοι.

Chapter XXIV

Passive Voice of the Participle
Supplementary Participles

Passive Participles

The future passive and aorist passive participles are formed on the sixth of the principal parts:

First Aorist Passive of λύω

Singular

	Mas.	Fem.	Neuter
N. & V.	λυθείς	λυθεῖσα	λυθέν
Gen.	λυθέντος	λυθείσης	λυθέντος
Dat.	λυθέντι	λυθείσῃ	λυθέντι
Acc.	λυθέντα	λυθεῖσαν	λυθέν

Plural

	Mas.	Fem.	Neuter
N. & V.	λυθέντες	λυθεῖσαι	λυθέντα
Gen.	λυθέντων	λυθεισῶν	λυθέντων
Dat.	λυθεῖσι (ν)	λυθείσαις	λυθεῖσι (ν)
Acc.	λυθέντας	λυθείσας	λυθέντα

Second Aorist Passive of γράφω

	Mas.	Fem.	Neuter
N. & V.	γραφείς	γραφεῖσα	γραφέν
Gen.	γραφέντος	γραφείσης	γραφέντος
Dat.	γραφέντι	γραφείσῃ	γραφέντι
Acc.	γραφέντα	γραφεῖσαν	γραφέν

Plural

	Mas.	Fem.	Neuter
N. & V.	γραφέντες	γραφεῖσαι	γραφέντα
Gen.	γραφέντων	γραφεισῶν	γραφέντων
Dat.	γραφεῖσι (ν)	γραφείσαις	γραφεῖσι (ν)
Acc.	γραφέντας	γραφείσας	γραφέντα

Future Passive of λύω
Singular

	Mas.	Fem.	Neuter
N. & V.	λυθησόμενος	λυθησομένη	λυθησόμενον
Gen.	λυθησομένου	λυθησομένης	λυθησομένου
Dat.	λυθησομένῳ	λυθησομένῃ	λυθησομένῳ
Acc.	λυθησόμενον	λυθησομένην	λυθησόμενον

Plural

	Mas.	Fem.	Neuter
N. & V.	λυθησόμενοι	λυθησόμεναι	λυθησόμενα
Gen.	λυθησομένων	λυθησομενῶν	λυθησομένων
Dat.	λυθησομένοις	λυθησομέναις	λυθησομένοις
Acc.	λυθησομένους	λυθησομένας	λυθησόμενα

The present and perfect passive participles have the same forms as their corresponding middle participles: λυόμενος is either a present middle or a present passive participle and λελυμένος is either a perfect middle or a perfect passive participle. In such instances the context indicates the voice.

Supplementary Participles

The supplementary participle stands in the predicate position. Its function is to complete or supplement the meaning of the governing verb. It does this by showing that to which the action of the verb relates. Unlike the attributive or circumstantial participles, the removal of the supplementary participle alters the meaning of its sentence. When the governing verb is intransitive or transitive passive, the supplementary participle modifies the subject of the verb. When the verb is transitive active, it modifies the object of the verb.

Periphrastic Participles

In the New Testament the supplementary participle occurs most frequently in periphrastic constructions. This construction usually consists of a verb form of εἰμι and either a present or a perfect participle. The following illustrations show the pattern that is used in forming the various tenses of the periphrastic participle and also show that the tenses of the periphrastic are translated like the corresponding tenses of the simple verb:

(1) The present periphrastic has the present of εἰμι and the present participle.

λέγει αὐτῇ, 'Ταλιθα κουμ', ὅ ἐστιν μεθερμηνευόμενον Τὸ κοράσιον (Mark 5:41); "He said [historical present] to her, 'Talitha Koum,' which **is translated** 'Damsel.'"

(2) The imperfect periphrastic has the imperfect of εἰμι and the present participle.

ἦν γὰρ **διδάσκων** αὐτούς (Mark 1:22); "For he **was teaching** them."

(3) The future periphrastic has the future of εἰμι and the present participle.
οἱ ἀστέρες **ἔσονται** ἐκ τοῦ οὐρανοῦ **πίπτοντες** (Mark 13:25); "The stars **will be falling** out of heaven."

(4) The perfect periphrastic has the present of εἰμι and the perfect participle.
ἐμνήσθησαν οἱ μαθηταὶ αὐτοῦ ὅτι **γεγραμμένον ἐστίν** (John 2:17); "His disciples remembered that is **was written**."

(5) The past perfect periphrastic has the imperfect of εἰμι and the perfect participle.

ἦν ὅλη ἡ πόλις **ἐπισυνηγμένη** πρὸς τὴν θύραν (Mark 1:33); "The whole city **had gathered** to the door."

(6) The future perfect periphrastic has the future of εἰμι and the perfect participle.

ἔσομαι πεποιθὼς ἐπ' αὐτῷ (Hebrews 2:13); "**I shall have been persuaded** by him."

Supplementary Participles after Certain Verbs

Some verbs require help in completing their verbal meaning. The supplementary participle, particularly in Classical Greek, may supply this help.

ξένος ἐτύγχανον **ὤν** (The Apology I:33); "I was happening **to be** a stranger."

ἔτυχον γὰρ **προσελθὼν** ἀνδρί (The Apology IV:15); "For I happened **to meet** a man."

The supplementary participle sometimes occurs after verbs of perception and may be translated as a dependent statement or noun clause.

εἶδεν **σχιζομένους** τοὺς οὐρανούς (Mark 1:10); "He saw that the heavens **were being divided**."

ἔλεγον αὐτῷ οἱ μαθηταὶ αὐτοῦ, Βλέπεις τὸν ὄχλον **συνθλίβοντά** σε, καὶ λέγεις, Τίς μου ἥψατο; (Mark 5:31); "His disciples were saying to him, 'You see that the multitude is pressing upon you, and you say, "Who is touching me?"'"

Vocabulary

1. ἀγρός, οῦ, ὁ — field (agriculture)
2. ἄρτι, adverb — now
3. ἰδέ and ἰδού — look or behold
   [imperative forms of εἶδον that are translated as interjections]
4. καινός, ή, όν — new
5. καλῶς, adverb — well
6. μαρτυρία, ας, ἡ — testimony (martyrology)
7. μάρτυς, μάρτυρος, ὁ — witness (martyr)
8. μνημεῖον, ου, τό — tomb
9. ὀλίγος, η, ον — little or few (oligarchy)
10. οὐαί, interjection — woe or alas
11. πάντοτε, adverb — always
12. πρόβατον, ου, τό — sheep
13. χωρίς, adverb — without
    followed by the gen.
14. δικαιόω, δικαιώσω, ἐδικαίωσα, δεδικαίωκα, δεδικαίωμαι, ἐδικαιώθην, justify
15. ἐπιτίθημι, ἐπιθήσω, ἐπέθηκα, ἐπιτέθεικα, ἐπιτέθειμαι, ἐπετέθην, lay upon, (epithet)
16. ἐργάζομαι, ἐργάσομαι, εἰργασάμην, --, εἴργασμαι, --, work, (ἔργον)
17. ἑτοιμάζω, ἑτοιμάσω, ἡτοίμασα, ἡτοίμακα, ἡτοίμασμαι, ἡτοιμάσθην, prepare, (ἕτοιμος)
18. εὐχαριστέω, εὐχαριστήσω, εὐχαρίστησα, εὐχαρίστηκα, εὐχαρίστημαι, εὐχαριστήθην, give thanks, (Eucharist)
19. θαυμάζω, θαυμάσομαι, ἐθαύμασα, τεθαύμακα, --, ἐθαυμάσθην, marvel or marvel at
20. τυγχάνω, τεύξομαι, ἔτυχον, τετύχηκα, --, --, happen or obtain

Exercise

Classify and translate the participles in the first three chapters of Mark.

Chapter XXV

The Imperative Mood

Form

The personal endings for the imperative are:

	Active		Middle and Passive	
	Singular	Plural	Singular	Plural
2.	θι	τε	σο	σθε
3.	τω	τωσαν	σθω	σθωσαν*

In the majority of the conjugations, the second person singular of all three voices is altered; hence, it is best to make this particular form in each conjugation a matter of special study.

The imperative occurs in the present, aorist, and perfect tenses. However, the perfect imperative is used so seldom that it will not be discussed in this text. Study the following present and aorist conjugations:

Present Imperative Conjugation of λύω

	Active		Middle and Passive	
	Singular	Plural	Singular	Plural
2.	λῦε	λύετε	λύου	λύεσθε
3.	λυέτω	λυέτωσαν	λυέσθω	λυέσθωσαν

Present Imperative Conjugation of δίδωμι

	Active		Middle and Passive	
	Singular	Plural	Singular	Plural
2.	δίδου	δίδοτε	δίδοσο	δίδοσθε
3.	διδότω	διδότωσαν	διδόσθω	διδόσθωσαν

---

* During the early period of Clasical Greek, the third person plural endings were ντων and σθων rather than τωσαν and σθωσαν.

Present Imperative Conjugation of ἵστημι

	Active		Middle and Passive	
	Singular	Plural	Singular	Plural
2.	ἵστη	ἵστατε	ἵστασο	ἵστασθε
3.	ἱστάτω	ἱστάτωσαν	ἱστάσθω	ἱστάσθωσαν

Present Imperative Conjugation of φιλέω

	Active		Middle and Passive	
	Singular	Plural	Singular	Plural
2.	φίλει	φιλεῖτε	φιλοῦ	φιλεῖσθε
3.	φιλείτω	φιλείτωσαν	φιλείσθω	φιλείσθωσαν

Present Imperative Conjugation of εἰμι

	Singular	Plural
2.	ἴσθι	ἔστε
3.	ἔστω	ἔστωσαν

First Aorist Imperative Conjugation of λύω

	Active		Middle	
	Singular	Plural	Singular	Plural
2.	λῦσον	λύσατε	λῦσαι	λύσασθε
3.	λυσάτω	λυσάτωσαν	λυσάσθω	λυσάσθωσαν

First Aorist Passive Imperative Conjugation of λύω

	Singular	Plural
2.	λύθητι	λύθητε
3.	λυθήτω	λυθήτωσαν

First Aorist Imperative Conjugation of μένω

	Active		Middle	
	Singular	Plural	Singular	Plural
2.	μεῖνον	μείνατε	μεῖναι	μείνασθε
3.	μεινάτω	μεινάτωσαν	μεινάσθω	μεινάσθωσαν

Second Aorist Imperative Conjugation of λαμβάνω

	Active		Middle	
	Singular	Plural	Singular	Plural
2.	λάβε	λάβετε	λαβοῦ	λάβεσθε
3.	λαβέτω	λαβέτωσαν	λαβέσθω	λαβέσθωσαν

Second Aorist Imperative Conjugation of δίδωμι

	Active		Middle	
	Singular	Plural	Singular	Plural
2.	δός	δότε	δοῦ	δόσθε
3.	δότω	δότωσαν	δόσθω	δόσθωσαν

Second Aorist Imperative Conjugation of ἵστημι

	Active		Middle	
	Singular	Plural	Singular	Plural
2.	στῆθι	στῆτε	στάσο	στάσθε
3.	στήτω	στήτωσαν	στάσθω	στάσθωσαν

Function

The imperative is the mood of command or request. Since the action of the command or request may or may not be carried out, it is a potential mood. As with all potential moods, the tense is timeless and expresses kind of action. The significance of voice for the imperative is the same as that for the indicative. If a verb is deponent in the indicative, it is also deponent in the imperative.

Neither English nor Greek has a first person imperative and both have a second person:

φιμώθητι καὶ ἔξελθε ἐξ αὐτοῦ (Mark 1:25); "**Be silent** and **come out** of him."

Ἐτοιμάσατε τὴν ὁδὸν κυρίου, εὐθείας ποεῖτε τὰς τρίβους αὐτοῦ (Mark 1:3); "**Prepare** the way of the Lord, **make** straight his paths."

In the latter illustration ἑτοιμάσατε is aorist and expresses undefined action; ποιεῖτε is present and expresses continuous action. Even though the distinction between the tenses is real ("Prepare" for ἑτοιμάσατε and "go through the process of making" for ποεῖτε), English translations seldom differentiate between the aorist and the present imperatives. Moreover, in English the subject of an imperative is rarely expressed ("Go," not "You go.") except for emphasis.

Unlike English, Greek has a third person imperative. The meaning of this construction may be expressed by using the imperative of the verb "let" and the infinitive of the Greek verb:

ὁ ἀναγινώσκων νοείτω (Mark 13:14); "**Let** the one who is reading **understand**."

εἰ δὲ τότε ἐπελάθετο, νῦν **παρασχέσθω**, ἐγὼ παραχωρῶ, καὶ **λεγέτω** (The Apology XXII:35-36); "But if he forgot it then, **let** him **do** so now; I myself yield the floor, and **let** him **speak**."

ἐλθέτω ἡ βασιλεία σου (Matthew 6:10); "**let** your kingdom **come**."

μή is the negative used with the imperative. In prohibitions (negative commands) the imperative mood normally uses the present tense. Here particularly the force of the present tense is seen, because prohibition expressed by the present imperative generally* means to stop an action that is in progress:

μὴ φοβοῦ, μόνον πίστευε (Mark 5:36); "**Stop fearing**, only believe."

μή μου **ἅπτου**, οὔπω γὰρ ἀναβέβηκα πρὸς πατέρα (John 20:17); "**Stop clinging** to me, for I have not yet ascended to the father."

μὴ θορυβεῖτε (The Apology XVIII:1); "**Stop making a disturbance**."

Vocabulary

1. ἄχρι and ἄχρις, conj.   until
   adverb followed by gen.   as far as
2. βιβλίον, ου, τό   book   (Bible)
3. διαθήκη, ης, ἡ   covenant
4. διακονία, ας, ἡ   ministry
5. διάκονος, ου, ὁ   servant   (deacon)
6. ἐγγύς, adverb   near   (ἐγγίζω)
7. ἐχθρός, ά, όν   hating
8. ὀπίσω, adverb   behind or after   (opisthograph)
   followed by the gen.
9. οὖς, ὠτός, τό   ear
10. προσευχή, ῆς, ἡ   prayer
11. πτωχός, ή, όν   poor
12. τιμή, ῆς, ἡ   honor or price   (Timothy)
13. ὥσπερ, adverb   just as
14. κατοικέω, κατοικήσω, κατῴκησα, --, --, --, inhabit, (οἶκος)
15. κλαίω, κλαύσομαι, ἔκλαυσα, --, κέκλαυσμαι, --, weep
16. λογίζομαι, λογίσομαι, ἐλογισάμην, --, λελόγισμαι, ἐλογίσθην, count or calculate, (apologize)
17. μισέω, μισήσω, ἐμίσησα, μεμίσηκα, μεμίσημαι, ἐμισήθην, hate, (misogamy)

---

* The context, on occasions, indicates that the command is: "Don't have a habit."

18. οἰκοδομέω, οἰκοδομήσω, ᾠκοδόμησα, --, ᾠκοδόμημαι, ᾠκοδομήθην, build, (οἶκος)

19. παραγίγνομαι or παραγίνομαι, παραγενήσομαι, παρεγενόμην, παραγέγονα, παραγεγένημαι, παρεγενήθην, come or arrive

20. σταυρόω, σταυρώσω, ἐσταύρωσα, ἐσταύρωκα, ἐσταύρωμαι, ἐσταυρώθην, crucify, (staurolite)

Translation

Mark 4:1-7

1 πλεῖστος (very large) ἐμβάντα (ἐμβαίνω) 2 πολλά (many things) 4 ὃ μὲν (some) 5 πολλήν (much)

The Apology I:1-9*

1 Ὅ τι (ὅστις, how) ὑμεῖς, ὦ ἄνδρες Ἀθηναῖοι, πεπόνθατε (πάσχω, to be affected) 2 ὑπὸ τῶν ἐμῶν κατηγόρων, οὐκ οἶδα· 3 ἐγὼ δ᾽ οὖν καὶ αὐτὸς ὑπ᾽ αὐτῶν ὀλίγου (almost) 4 ἐμαυτοῦ ἀπελαθόμην (ἐπιλανθάνομαι)· οὕτω πιθανῶς (persuasively) ἔλεγον. 5 καί τοι (yet) ἀληθές γε, ὡς, ἔπος εἰπεῖν, 6 οὐδὲν εἰρήκασιν. μάλιστα δὲ αὐτῶν ἓν ἐθαύμασα 7 τῶν πολλῶν (many) ὧν ἐψεύσαντο. τοῦτο ἐν ᾧ ἔλεγον ὡς (that) 8 χρὴ (it is necessary) ὑμᾶς εὐλαβεῖσθαι, μὴ (lest) ὑπ᾽ ἐμοῦ ἐξαπατηθῆτε (you be deceived) 9 ὡς δεινοῦ (δεινός, ή, όν, clever) ὄντος λέγειν.

Luke 18:16

ὁ δὲ Ἰησοῦς προσεκαλέσατο αὐτὰ λέγων, Ἄφετε τὰ παιδία ἔρχεσθαι πρός με καὶ μὴ κωλύετε αὐτά.

James 5:14

ἀσθενεῖ τις ἐν ὑμῖν; προσκαλεσάσθω τοὺς πρεσβυτέρους τῆς ἐκκλησίας, καὶ προσευξάσθωσαν ἐπ᾽ αὐτὸν ἀλείψαντες αὐτὸν ἐλαίῳ ἐν τῷ ὀνόματι τοῦ κυρίου.

---

* Vocabulary words not listed in Barclay M. Newman, Jr., *A Concise Greek-English Dictionary of the New Testament* (London: United Bible Societies, 1971) are given in the parentheses.

John 1:29

τῇ ἐπαύριον βλέπει τὸν Ἰησοῦν ἐρχόμενον πρὸς αὐτόν.

Acts 7:56

καὶ εἶπεν, Ἰδού θεωρῶ τοὺς οὐρανοὺς διηνοιγμένους καὶ τὸν υἱὸν τοῦ ἀνθρώπου ἐκ δεξιῶν ἑστῶτα τοῦ θεοῦ.

Chapter XXVI

The Subjunctive Mood in Independent Clauses

Form

The present and aorist tenses, rarely the perfect, are used in the subjunctive mood. The tenses of this mood use primary endings which are suffixed to the appropriate principal part with a lengthened variable vowel:

Present Subjunctive Conjugation of λύω

	Active		Middle and Passive	
	Singular	Plural	Singular	Plural
1.	λύω	λύωμεν	λύωμαι	λυώμεθα
2.	λύῃς	λύητε	λύῃ	λύησθε
3.	λύῃ	λύωσι (ν)	λύηται	λύωνται

Present Subjunctive Conjugation of δίδωμι

	Active		Middle and Passive	
	Singular	Plural	Singular	Plural
1.	διδῶ	διδῶμεν	διδῶμαι	διδώμεθα
2.	διδῷς	διδῶτε	διδῷ	διδῶσθε
3.	διδῷ	διδῶσι (ν)	διδῶται	διδῶνται

Present Subjunctive Conjugation of ἵστημι

	Active		Middle and Passive	
	Singular	Plural	Singular	Plural
1.	ἱστῶ	ἱστῶμεν	ἱστῶμαι	ἱστώμεθα
2.	ἱστῇς	ἱστῆτε	ἱστῇ	ἱστῆσθε
3.	ἱστῇ	ἱστῶσι (ν)	ἱστῆται	ἱστῶνται

Present Subjunctive Conjugation of εἰμι

	Singular	Plural
1.	ὦ	ὦμεν
2.	ᾖς	ἦτε
3.	ᾖ	ὦσι (ν)

Present Subjunctive Conjugation of φιλέω

	Active		Middle and Passive	
	Singular	Plural	Singular	Plural
1.	φιλῶ	φιλῶμεν	φιλῶμαι	φιλώμεθα
2.	φιλῇς	φιλῆτε	φιλῇ	φιλῆσθε
3.	φιλῇ	φιλῶσι (ν)	φιλῆται	φιλῶνται

First Aorist Subjunctive Conjugation of λύω

	Active		Middle	
	Singular	Plural	Singular	Plural
1.	λύσω	λύσωμεν	λύσωμαι	λυσώμεθα
2.	λύσῃς	λύσητε	λύσῃ	λύσησθε
3.	λύσῃ	λύσωσι (ν)	λύσηται	λύσωνται

First Aorist Passive Subjunctive Conjugation of λύω

	Singular	Plural
1.	λυθῶ	λυθῶμεν
2.	λυθῇς	λυθῆτε
3.	λυθῇ	λυθῶσι (ν)

Second Aorist Conjugation of λάμβανω

	Singular	Plural	Singular	Plural
1.	λάβω	λάβωμεν	λάβωμαι	λαβώμεθα
2.	λάβῃς	λάβητε	λάβῃ	λάβησθε
3.	λάβῃ	λάβωσι (ν)	λάβηται	λάβωνται

The second aorist subjunctive conjugations of δίδωμι and ἵστημι are the same as their present conjugations, except there is no reduplication: δῶ and στῶ.

Function

The subjunctive is a potential mood, and the difference in tenses again is a difference in kind of action. The significance of voice for the subjunctive is the same as for the indicative, and a verb that is deponent in the indicative is also deponent in the subjunctive.

The subjunctive is used in certain special constructions, and the particular construction determines how the subjunctive will be translated. Consequently, there is no one translation that will suffice for every time that the subjunctive occurs.

In this chapter, four uses of the subjunctive are considered. In each of these uses the subjunctive is the predicate in an independent clause.*

Deliberative

The subjunctive used in a question indicates that the answer to this question is to be a command.

τί αἰτήσωμαι; (Mark 6:24); "What **shall I ask?**"

ἀλλὰ δὴ φυγῆς τιμήσωμαι; (The Apology XXVII:24-24); "So **shall I propose** exile as a penalty?"

Emphatic Negation

The aorist subjunctive may be used after the double negative οὐ μή to make a strong or emphatic negative statement.

οὐ μὴ ἀφεθῇ ὧδε λίθος ἐπὶ λίθον ὃς **οὐ μὴ καταλυθῇ** (Mark 13:2); "There **shall not in anywise be left** here stone upon stone, which **shall not be thrown down.**"

θάνατον **οὐ μὴ θεωρήσῃ** (John 8:51); "He **shall never see** death."

οὐ μὴ παύσωμαι φιλοσοφῶν (The Apology XXVII:44); "**I shall never give up** philosophy."

Hortatory

The first person plural (occasionally the singular in Classical Greek) of the subjunctive may be used to make a request or proposal.

ἄγωμεν ἀλλαχοῦ (Mark 1:38); "**Let us go** elsewhere."

ἀναλάβωμεν οὖν ἐξ ἀρχῆς (The Apology III:1); "Then **let us take up** from the beginning."

Prohibition

The aorist subjunctive is used in negative commands to prohibit an act before it begins.

μηδὲν εἴπῃς (Mark 1:44); "**Do not say** anything."

μὴ θορυβήσητε (The Apology V:21-22); "**Do not make a disturbance.**"

---

* These uses may also occur in certain dependent clauses.

Vocabulary

1. ἀληθινός, ή, όν — real or true (ἀλήθεια)
2. ἄνεμος, ου, ὁ — wind (anemone)
3. ἀρνίον, ου, τό — lamb
4. γε, enclitic particle*
5. διδαχή, ῆς, ἡ — teaching (didactic)
6. δυνατός, ή, όν — able or strong (dynamic)
7. ἥλιος, ου, ὁ — sun (helium)
8. καί, adverb — also or even
9. μέλος, ους, τό — limb or song (melody)
10. οἶνος, ου, ὁ — wine (oenologist)
11. ποῖος, α, ον interrogative adjective — what kind of
12. ποτήριον, ου, τό — cup
13. σκότος, ους, τό — darkness (skotophobia)
14. ὑπομονή, ῆς, ἡ — steadfastness
15. ἀσθενέω, --, ἠσθένησα, ἠσθένηκα, --, --, be sick, (asthenosphere)
16. βούλομαι, βουλήσομαι, --, --, βεβούλημαι, ἐβουλήθην, wish, (bouleterion)
17. ἐπιστρέφω, ἐπιστρέψω, ἐπέστρεψα, ἐπέστροφα, ἐπέστραμμαι, ἐπεστράφην, turn or return, (catastrophe)
18. πάσχω, πείσομαι, ἔπαθον, πέπονθα, --, --, suffer, (pathetic)
19. περισσεύω, περισσεύσω, ἐπερίσσευσα, --, --, ἐπερισσεύθην, abound, (perissodactyle)
20. πλανάω, πλανήσω, ἐπλάνησα, --, πεπλάνημαι, ἐπλανήθην, lead astray, (planet)

Translation

Mark 4:8-12

12 βλέπωσιν (they may see) ἴδωσιν (they may see) ἀκούωσιν (they may hear) συνιῶσιν (they may understand) ἐπιστρέψωσιν (they may return) ἀφεθῇ (it may be forgiven)

---

* Particle is a general term for any small word which is indeclinable. Thus the negative adverbs, other adverbs, prepositions, interjections, and conjunctions are sometimes called particles. This text, however, designates as particles those small words which express shades of meaning often untranslatable in English. These words usually add emphasis to the word with which they are associated.

Apology I:9-17

9 τὸ γὰρ μὴ αἰσχυνθῆναι, ὅτι 10 αὐτίκα (instantly) ὑπ' ἐμοῦ ἐξελεγχθήσονται (ἐκελέγχω, refute) ἔργῳ, ἐπειδὰν (after that) μηδ' 11 ὁπωστιοῦν (in anyway so ever) φαίνωμαι (I am found) δεινὸς (δεινός, ή, όν, clever) λέγειν, τοῦτό μοι ἔδοξεν 12 αὐτῶν ἀναισχυντότατον (most shameless) εἶναι, εἰ μὴ (unless) ἄρα (perhaps) δεινὸν (clever) 13 καλοῦσιν οὗτοι λέγειν τὸν τἀληθῆ (τά + ἀληθῆ, object of λέγοντα) λέγοντα· εἰ μὲν 14 γὰρ τοῦτο λέγουσιν, ὁμολογοίην ἂν ἔγωγ' (translate the three preceding words: "I myself would confess") οὐ κατὰ 15 τούτους εἶναι ῥήτωρ. οὗτοι μὲν οὖν, ὥσπερ ἐγὼ 16 λέγω, ἤ τι ἢ οὐδὲν (translate the four preceding words "little or nothing") ἀληθὲς εἰρήκασιν· ὑμεῖς δέ μου 17 ἀκούσεσθε πᾶσαν τὴν ἀλήθειαν.

I Cor 11:22

τί εἴπω ὑμῖν;

Acts 18:9

Μὴ φοβοῦ, ἀλλὰ λάλει καὶ μὴ σιωπήσῃς.

Luke 6:37

μὴ κρίνετε, καὶ οὐ μὴ κριθῆτε.

I Cor 15:32

Φάγωμεν καὶ πίωμεν.

Chapter XXVII

The Subjunctive Mood in Dependent Clauses
Conditional Sentences

The Subjunctive Mood in Dependent Clauses

<u>Purpose Clauses</u>

The subjunctive may be used in a dependent clause to express purpose. ἵνα or ὅπως usually introduce this clause.

> ἄγωμεν εἰς τὰς ἐχομένας κωμοπόλεις, ἵνα καὶ ἐκεῖ **κηρύξω** (Mark 1:38); "Let us go into the neighboring towns, **in order that I may** also **preach** there."

> ἀκούαστε δή μου . . ., **ἵνα εἴδητε** ὅτι οὐδ' ἂν ἑνὶ ὑπεικάθοιμι (The Apology XX:3-5); "Hear me now . . ., **in order that you may see** that I would never yield to anyone."

> οἱ φαρισαῖοι . . . συμβούλιον ἐδίδουν κατ' αὐτοῦ ὅπως αὐτὸν ἀπολέσωσιν (Mark 3:6); "The Pharisees . . . were giving counsel against him **in order that** they **might kill** him."

If the purpose clause is negative, it is most frequently introduced by ἵνα μή.

> προσεύχεσθε **ἵνα μὴ ἔλθητε** εἰς πειρασμόν (Mark 14:38); "Pray **in order that** you **may not come** into temptation."

> λέγε οὖν ἡμῖν, τί ἐστιν, ἵνα μὴ ἡμεῖς περὶ σοῦ **αὐτοσχεδιάζωμεν** (The Apology V:7-8); "Therefore tell us, what it is, **in order that we may not act unadvisedly** concerning you."

<u>Object Clauses</u>

Verbs of striving, beseeching, or commanding may be followed by a subjunctive clause which is introduced by ἵνα. In meaning these clauses are closely related to indicative clauses that are introduced by ὅτι.

οὐκ ἤφιεν **ἵνα** τις **διενέγκῃ** σκεῦος διὰ τοῦ ἱεροῦ (Mark 11:16); "He was not permitting **that** any **should carry** a vessel through the temple."

αὕτη ἐστὶν ἡ ἐντολὴ ἡ ἐμή, **ἵνα ἀγαπᾶτε** ἀλλήλους (John 15:12); "This is my commandment, **that** you **love** one another."

Object clauses after verbs of fearing or caution are introduced by μή, and in this construction it is translated "lest."

βλέπετε **μή** τις ὑμᾶς **πλανήσῃ** (Mark 13:5); "Watch, **lest** anyone **leads you astray**."

ἔλεγον ὡς χρὴ ὑμᾶς εὐλαβεῖσθαι **μὴ** ὑπ᾽ ἐμοῦ **ἐξαπατηθῆτε** (The Apology I:7-8); "They were saying that it was necessary that you be cautious **lest you be utterly deceived** by me."

Conditional Relative Clauses

A relative clause that refers to a potential event or instance has a subjunctive verb and ἄν (occasionally ἐάν).

οἷός τ᾽ ἐστίν... ξυνεῖναι **ᾧ ἂν βούλωνται** (The Apology IV:8-11); "It is possible... to associate with **whomever** they **wish**."

ἀφεθήσεται... αἱ βλασφημίαι **ὅσα ἐὰν βλασφημήσωσιν· ὃς δ᾽ ἂν βλασφημήσῃ** εἰς τὸ πνεῦμα τὸ ἅγιον οὐκ ἔχει ἄφεσιν (Mark 3:28-29); "The blasphemies .. **as many as** they **may blaspheme** will be forgiven; but **whoever blasphemes** against the Holy Spirit is not having forgiveness."

Conditional Temporal Clauses

A temporal clause denotes the time of the action in its independent clause. These clauses are introduced by adverbs such as ὅτε and ἕως. When the time denoted is indefinite, the temporal clause usually contains a subjunctive verb and the particle ἄν.

ὁ υἱὸς τοῦ ἀνθρώπου ἐπαισχυνθήσεται αὐτὸν **ὅταν* ἔλθῃ** ἐν τῇ δόξῃ τοῦ πατρὸς αὐτοῦ (Mark 8:38); "The son of man will be ashamed of him **whenever** he **comes** in his father's glory."

ἑώρακά τινας, **ὅταν κρίνωνται** (The Apology XXII:34-35); "**Whenever** they **are judged**, I have seen some."

χρημάτων, καὶ δεδέσθαι, **ἕως ἂν ἐκτίσω**; (The Apology XXVII:17); "[Shall I propose] to be imprisoned with a fine **until I pay**?"

---

* ὅταν is a contraction of ὅτε and ἄν.

λέγω ὑμῖν ὅτι εἰσίν τινες ὧδε τῶν ἑστηκότων οἵτινες οὐ μὴ γεύσωνται θανάτου **ἕως ἂν ἴδωσιν** τὴν βασιλείαν (Mark 9:1); "I say to you that there are some of those who stand here who will never taste death **until** they **see** the kingdom.

Contrast this subjunctive temporal clause with the following indicative temporal clause in which the verb points to a specific time (the dismissing of the crowd).

ἠνάγκασεν τοὺς μαθητὰς αὐτοῦ ἐμβῆναι εἰς τὸ πλοῖον . . . **ἕως** αὐτὸς **ἀπολύει** τὸν ὄχλον (Mark 6:45); "He urged his disciples to go into the boat . . . **while** (until) he himself **dismissed** the multitude."

Conditional Sentences

Conditional sentences assert that something will happen if something else happens. In its simplest form it consists of a subordinate clause that expressed the condition (protasis) and the main clause that expresses the conclusion (apodosis). Conditional sentences show great variety of form, but it will suffice for this book to discuss four classes of condition.

Simple Condition

This condition affirms the reality of the protasis. εἰ occurs regularly in the protasis with any tense of the indicative. The apodosis may have any mood or tense.

εἰ ὁ Σατανᾶς **ἀνέστη** ἐφ' ἑαυτὸν καὶ **ἐμερίσθη**, οὐ δύναται στῆναι (Mark 3:26); "**If** (since) Satan **has risen** against himself and **was divided**, he is not able to stand."

εἰ οὖν τοιοῦτον ὁ θάνατός **ἐστιν**, κέρδος ἔγωγε λέγω (The Apology XXXII:19-20); "Therefore, **if** (since) such **is** death, I myself say [it is] gain."

Contrary to Fact Condition

In this condition the protasis indicates that the condition was not fulfilled. The apodosis states what would have been if the protasis had been fulfilled. The protasis is introduced by εἰ and has a past tense of the indicative mood. The apodosis has the past tense of the indicative and usually ἄν.

εἰ μὴ **ἐκολόβωσεν** κύριος τὰς ἡμέρας, οὐκ **ἂν ἐσώθη** πᾶσα σάρξ (Mark 13:20); "**If** the Lord **had** not **shortened** the days, no flesh **would have been saved**."

εἰ ἦς ὧδε οὐκ ἄν μου ἀπέθανεν ὁ ἀδελφός (John 11:32); "**If you had been** here, my brother **would** not **have died.**"

εἰ μέν σου τὼ υἱέε πώλω ἢ μόσχω ἐγενέσθην, εἴχομεν ἂν αὐτοῖν ἐπιστάτην λαβεῖν (The Apology IV:18-20); "**If** your two sons **had been** colts or calves, we **should be able** to take for them an overseer."

Probable Future Condition

ἐάν introduces the protasis of the probable future condition, and the verb of this protasis has the subjunctive mood. The verb of the apodosis may have any form as long as it has to do with the future. The condition in this type of sentence has not been fulfilled but probably will be.

ἐὰν βασιλεία ἐφ' ἑαυτὴν **μερισθῇ** οὐ δύναται σταθῆναι ἡ βασιλεία ἐκείνη (Mark 3:24); "**If** a kingdom **is divided** against itself, that kingdom is not able to stand."

ἐὰν ἅψωμαι... τῶν ἱματίων αὐτοῦ σωθήσομαι (Mark 5:28); "**If I touch**... his garments, I shall be saved."

ἐὰν δοκῶσί τι εἶναι μηδὲν ὄντες, ὀνειδίζετε αὐτοῖς (The Apology XXXIII:18-19); "**If** they **think** that they are something while being nothing, reproach them."

Less Probable Future Condition

This condition is farther from reality than the probable future condition. It uses the optative (see Chapter XXIX) in both the protasis and apodosis; ἄν is in the apodosis. This construction does not occur in its full form in the Septuagint or the New Testament; however, in the following example the understood words are supplied.

ἀλλ' **εἰ** καὶ **πάσχοιτε** διὰ δικαιοσύνην, μακάριοι [**ἂν εἴητε**] (I Peter 3:14); "But even **if** you **should suffer** because of righteousness, [you **would be**] happy."

The less probable future condition does occur in Classical Greek.

θαυμάζοιμ' **ἂν εἰ** οἷός τ' **εἴην** ἐγὼ ὑμῶν ταύτην τὴν διαβολὴν ἐξελέσθαι (The Apology X:27-29); "**I should marvel** if I **were** able to remove this prejudice from you."

ὁμοίως γὰρ **ἂν** ἄτοπον **εἴη**, ὥσπερ **ἂν** εἴ τις ἵππων μὲν παῖδας ἡγοῖτο (The Apology XV:33-34); "**It would be** just as absurd as if someone **were believing** that there are human offsprings of horses."

Vocabulary

1. ἄν, a particle, [this word makes a statement contingent which would otherwise be definite]
2. γνῶσις, γνώσεως, ἡ   knowledge   (prognosis)
3. ἐάν, conjunction   if
4. εἰ, conjunction   if or since
5. ἕως, conjunction   until or while
   prep. with gen.   as far as
6. ἵνα, conjunction   in order that or that
7. ναί, adverb   yes or certainly
8. ὁμοίως, adverb   likewise   (homily)
9. ὅπως, conjunction   in order that or that
10. παρρησία, ας, ἡ   boldness
11. περιτομή, ῆς, ἡ   circumcision
12. πλήν, conjunction   but or nevertheless
    prep. with gen.   except
13. συνείδησις, εως, ἡ   conscience
14. φυλή, ῆς, ἡ   tribe or nation   (phylogeny)
15. βλασφημέω, βλασφημήσω, ἐβλασφήμησα, βεβλασφήμηκα, βεβλασφήμημαι, ἐβλασφημήθην, blaspheme, (blaspheme)
16. μετανοέω, μετανοήσω, μετενόησα, --, -, --, repent, (noetics)
17. ὀφείλω, ὀφειλήσω, ὤφείλησα or ὤφελον, ὠφείληκα, --, ὠφειλήθην, owe or ought
18. πειράζω, --, ἐπείρασα, --, πεπείρασμαι, ἐπειράσθην, test or tempt
19. πράσσω or πράττω, πράξω, ἔπραξα, πέπραχα, πέπραγμαι, ἐπράχθην, do, (practice)
20. ὑποστρέφω, ὑποστρέψω, ὑπέστρεψα, ὑπέστροφα, ὑπέστραμμαι, ὑπεστράφην, return, (apostrophe)

Translation

Mark 4:13-18

The Apology I:17-26

17 οὐ μέντοι μὰ (particle used is oaths, "by") Δία (Ζεύς, Διός, ὁ, Zeus), 18 ὦ ἄνδρες Ἀθηναῖοι, κεκαλλιεπημένους (καλλιεπέομαι, speak in fine words) γε

λόγους, 19 ὥσπερ οἱ τούτων, ῥήμασί (ῥῆμα may be translated "phrase") τε καὶ ὀνόμασιν (ὄνομα may be translated "word") οὐδὲ 20 κεκοσμημένους, ἀλλ᾽ ἀκούσεσθε εἰκῇ (at random) λεγόμενα τοῖς 21 ἐπιτυχοῦσιν (ἐπιτυγχάνω, chanced upon) ὀνόμασιν· πιστεύω γὰρ δίκαια εἶναι ἃ 22 λέγω, καὶ μηδεὶς ὑμῶν προσδοκησάτω ἄλλως· οὐδὲ 23 γὰρ ἂν δήπου πρέποι (πρέπω, pres. act. opt. 3 s., be fit), ὦ ἄνδρες, τῇδε τῇ ἡλικίᾳ 24 ὥσπερ μειρακίῳ (μειράκιον, ου, τό, lad) πλάττοντι (πλάσσω) λόγους εἰς ὑμᾶς εἰσιέναι (εἴσειμι). 25 καὶ μέντοι (in truth) πάνυ (earnestly) ὦ ἄνδρες Ἀθηναῖοι, τοῦτο ὑμῶν 26 δέομαι καὶ παρίεμαι (παρίεμαι, entreat).

John 13:19

λέγω ὑμῖν . . ., ἵνα πιστεύσητε.

Mark 6:25

θέλω ἵνα . . . δῷς μοι . . . τὴν κεφαλὴν Ἰωάννου.

John 15:19

εἰ ἐκ τοῦ κόσμου ἦτε, ὁ κόσμος ἂν τὸ ἴδιον ἐφίλει.

I Cor. 13:11

ὅτε ἤμην νήπιος, ἐλάλουν ὡς νήπιος.

Matt. 15:2

οὐ γὰρ νίπτονται τὰς χεῖρας αὐτῶν ὅταν ἄρτον ἐσθίωσιν.

Matt 5:19

ὃς δ᾽ ἂν . . . διδάξῃ οὗτος μέγας (great) κληθήσεται.

Chapter XXVIII

Comparison of Adjectives

In comparing objects with each other in Greek, as in English we normally use three different forms of the same adjective. The three forms are called degrees of comparison: positive degree, comparative degree, and superlative degree.

Positive Degree

The positive degree merely describes without suggesting any comparison. ἀγαθός, ή, όν (Chapter IV) is an example of a positive adjective that is declined like the first and second declensions. ἀληθής, ές (Chapter XVIII) is a positive adjective that is declined like the third declension. The declension of αἰώνιος, ον, which follows the second declension, is as follows:

	Singular		Plural	
	Mas. & Fem.	Neuter	Mas. & Fem.	Neuter
Nom.	αἰώνιος	αἰώνιον	αἰώνιοι	αἰώνια
Gen.	αἰωνίου	αἰωνίου	αἰωνίων	αἰωνίων
Dat.	αἰωνίῳ	αἰωνίῳ	αἰνωνίοις	αἰωνίοις
Acc.	αἰώνιον	αἰώνιον	αἰωνίους	αἰώνια
Voc.	αἰώνιε	αἰώνιον	αἰώνιοι	αἰώνια

All adjectives whose masculine and feminine nominative singulars end with an "ος" and whose nominative neuter singular ends with an "ον" are declined like αἰώνιος, ον.

The declentions of μέγας, "great," and πόλυς, "many," differ somewhat from that of ἀγαθός. These adjectives are used so frequently that their declensions should be memorized.

	Singular			Plural		
	Mas.	Fem.	Neuter	Mas.	Fem.	Neuter
Nom.	μέγας	μεγάλη	μέγα	μεγάλοι	μεγάλαι	μεγάλα
Gen.	μεγάλου	μεγάλης	μεγάλου	μεγάλων	μεγάλων	μεγάλων
Dat.	μεγάλῳ	μεγάλῃ	μεγάλῳ	μεγάλοις	μεγάλαις	μεγάλοις
Acc.	μέγαν	μεγάλην	μέγα	μεγάλους	μεγάλας	μεγάλα
Voc.	μεγάλε	μεγάλη	μέγα	μεγάλοι	μεγάλαι	μεγάλα

	Singular			Plural		
	Mas.	Fem.	Neuter	Mas.	Fem.	Neuter
Nom.	πολύς	πολλή	πολύ	πολλοί	πολλαί	πολλά
Gen.	πολλοῦ	πολλῆς	πολλοῦ	πολλῶν	πολλῶν	πολλῶν
Dat.	πολλῷ	πολλῇ	πολλῷ	πολλοῖς	πολλαῖς	πολλοῖς
Acc.	πολύν	πολλήν	πολύ	πολλούς	πολλάς	πολλά

Observe:
1. The stems of μέγας and πολύς are found by dropping the genitive singular endings.
2. The accusative masculine singulars of both adjectives are irregular.

Comparative Degree

The comparative degree indicates that the attribute of the substantive described is in a higher degree than the substantive with which it is compared. In English the comparative degree is formed by suffixing "er" or by prefixing the adverb "more" to the positive adjective: holy becomes holier and beautiful becomes more beautiful. In Greek the comparative degree is formed by suffixing τερ or ιων (sometimes ων) to the positive degree of the adjective: δίκαιος, α, ον becomes δικαιότερος, α, ον; and the positive adjective ἡδύς, ἡδεία, ἡδύ* becomes ἡδίων, ἡδίον (the masculine and feminine are identical).

The following is the declension δικαιότερος:

	Singular		
	Mas.	Fem.	Neuter
Nom.	δικαιότερος	δικαιοτέρα	δικαιότερον
Gen.	δικαιοτέρου	δικαιοτέρας	δικαιοτέρου
Dat.	δικαιοτέρῳ	δικαιοτέρα	δικαιοτέρῳ
Acc.	δικαιότερον	δικαιοτέραν	δικαιότερον
Voc.	δικαιότερε	δικαοτέρα	δικαιότερον

---

* See appendix for the declension of ἡδύς.

Singular

	Mas.	Fem.	Neuter
Nom.	δικαιότεροι	δικαιότεραι	δικαιότερα
Gen.	δικαιοτέρων	δικαιοτέρων	δικαιοτέρων
Dat.	δικαιοτέροις	δικαιοτέραις	δικαιοτέροις
Acc.	δικαιοτέρους	δικαιοτέρας	δικαιότερα

The following is the declension of ἡδίων:

	Singular		Plural	
	Mas. & Fem.	Neuter	Mas. & Fem.	Neuter
N. & V.	ἡδίων	ἥδιον	ἡδίονες or ἡδίους	ἡδίονα or ἡδίω
Gen.	ἡδίονος	ἡδίονος	ἡδιόνων	ἡδιόνων
Dat.	ἡδίονι	ἡδίονι	ἡδίοσι (ν)	ἡδίοσι (ν)
Acc.	ἡδίονα or ἡδίω	ἥδιον	ἡδίονας or ἡδίους	ἡδίονα or ἡδίω

The comparative degree of a number of adjectives is formed on a different stem from that which their positive degree is formed; for example, μέγας, μεγάλη, μέγα becomes μείζων, ον. It is declined:

	Singular		Plural	
	Mas. & Fem.	Neuter	Mas. & Fem.	Neuter
N. & V.	μείζων	μεῖζον	μείζονες or μείζους	μείζονα or μείζω
Gen.	μείζονος	μείζονος	μειζόνων	μειζόνων
Dat.	μείζονι	μείζονι	μείζοσι (ν)	μείζοσι (ν)
Acc.	μείζονα or μείζω	μεῖζον	μείζονας or μείζους	μείζονα or μείζω

The comparative may be followed by the subordinate conjunction ἤ "than" and the substantive which is being compared. Both substantives must be in the same case.

μείζων ἐστὶν ὁ ἐν ὑμῖν ἢ ὁ ἐν τῷ κόσμῳ (I John 4:4); "**He** that is in you is **greater than he** that is in the world."

εὐκοπώτερόν ἐστιν κάμηλον ... ἢ πλούσιον (Mark 10:25); "It is **easier** for a **camel** ... **than a rich man**."

οὐκ ἐμὲ μείζω βλάψετε ἢ ὑμᾶς (The Apology XVIII:8-9); "You will not injure **me more than you**."

The substantive with which a comparison is made may be in the genitive case. This construction is called the genitive of comparison.

μείζων τούτων ἄλλη ἐντολὴ οὐκ ἔστιν (Mark 12:31); "No other commandment is **greater than these**."

τούτου μὲν τοῦ **ἀνθρώπου** ἐγὼ **σοφώτερός** εἰμι (The Apology VI: 24); "I myself am **wiser than this man**."

Superlative Degree

The superlative degree denotes that the attribute of the substantive described is in its highest degree. In English the superlative degree is formed by suffixing "est" or by prefixing the adverb "most:" holy becomes holiest and beautiful becomes most beautiful. In Greek positive adjectives which use the suffix τερ for the comparative degree use the suffix τατ for the superlative degree.

ἐποικοδομοῦντες ἑαυτοὺς τῇ **ἁγιωτάτῃ** ὑμῶν πίστει . . . ἑαυτοὺς ἐν ἀγάπῃ θεοῦ τηρήσατε (Jude 1:20-21); "Building up yourselves upon your **holiest** faith . . . keep yourselves in the love of God."

τοῦτό μοι ἔδοξεν αὐτῶν **ἀναισχυντότατον** εἶναι (The Apology I:11-12); "This seemed to me to be **most shameless** of them."

Positive adjectives which use the suffix ων or ιων for the comparative degree use the suffix ιστ for the superlative degree.

ἐγὼ γάρ εἰμι ὁ **ἐλάχιστος** τῶν ἀποστόλων (I Cor. 15:9): "For I myself am **least** of the apostles."

διὰ τὸ τὴν τέχνην καλῶς ἐξεργάζεσθαι ἕκαστος ἠξίου καὶ τἆλλα τὰ **μέγιστα** σοφώτατος εἶναι (The Apology VIII:9-10); "Because they were practicing their art well, each one thought that he was also wisest with reference to the other **most important matters**."

The superlative may indicate that the attribute of the substantive described is in a very high degree, and not necessarily in the highest degree. It is possible that this is the idea expressed by σοφώτατος in the illustration above. If this is the case, the sentence would be translated, "Because they were practicing their art well, each one thought that he was **very wise** with reference to the other most important matters." Study the following illustration from the New Testament:

συνάγεται πρὸς αὐτὸν ὄχλος **πλεῖστος** (Mark 4:1); "A **very large** crowd gathered to him."

Vocabulary

1. αἰώνιος, ον	eternal	(αἰών)
2. ἀκάθαρτος, ον	unclean	(catharsis)
3. ἁμαρτωλός, όν	sinful	(ἁμαρτία)

4. διάβολος, ον   slanderous   (diabolical)
   [used substantivally "Devil"]
5. ἕνεκα or ἕνεκεν, prep. with the gen., **because of**
   [the gen. substantive usually precedes this prep.]
6. κρίμα, κρίματος, τό   judgment   (criterion)
7. μέγας, μεγάλη, μέγα   great   (megaphone)
8. μείζων, ον   greater
   comparative of μέγας
9. μυστήριον, ου, τό   mystery   (mystery)
10. παράκλησις, εως, ἡ   comfort or help   (Paraklete)
11. πλείων, ον   more   (pleonasm)
    comparative of πολύς
12. πολύς, πολλή, πολύ   much or many   (polygon)
13. πότε, interrogative adv.   when
14. στρατιώτης, ου, ὁ   soldier   (strategy)
15. ἀρνέομαι, ἀρνήσομαι, ἠρνησάμην, --, ἤρνημαι, ἠρνήθην, deny
16. ἀγοράζω, ἀγοράσω, ἠγόρασα, ἠγόρακα, --, ἠγοράσθην, buy, (agoraphobia)
17. διακονέω, διακονήσω, ἐδιακόνησα, δεδιακόνηκα, δεδιακόνημαι, ἐδιακονήθην, serve
18. καυχάομαι, καυχήσομαι, ἐκαυχησάμην, --, κεκαύχημαι, --, boast
19. ὑποτάσσω, ὑποταγήσομαι, ὑπέταξα, --, ὑποτέταγμαι, ὑπετάγην, subject, (hypotaxis)
20. φυλάσσω or φυλάττω, φυλάξω, ἐφύλαξα πεφύλαχα, πεφύλαγμαι, ἐφυλάχθην, guard, (prophylactic)

Translation

Mark 4:19-23

21 τεθῇ (τίθημι)

The Apology I:26-37

26 ἐὰν διὰ τῶν αὐτῶν λόγων   27 ἀκούητέ μου ἀπολογουμένου, δι᾽ ὧνπερ (ὅσπερ) εἴωθα (ἔθω, perf. act. ind. 1 s., accustom) λέγειν   28 καὶ ἐν ἀγορᾷ ἐπὶ τῶν τραπεζῶν, ἵνα (where) ὑμῶν πολλοὶ   29 ἀκηκόασι, καὶ ἄλλοθι (elsewhere), μήτε (neither) θαυμάζειν μήτε (nor) θορυβεῖν   30 τούτου ἕνεκα. ἔχει γὰρ οὑτωσί (emphatic form of οὕτω). νῦν ἐγὼ πρῶτον   31 ἐπὶ δικαστήριον

(δικαστήριον, ου, τό, court of justice) ἀναβέβηκα, ἔτη γεγονὼς ἑβδομήκοντα· 32 ἀτεχνῶς (utterly) οὖν ξένως (adverb with the genitive "ignorant of") ἔχω τῆς ἐνθάδε λέξεως (λέξις, εως, ἡ, style of speech). 33 ὥσπερ οὖν ἄν, εἰ τῷ ὄντι (translate the preceding substantival participle "in truth") ξένος ἐτύγχανον ὤν, 34 ξυνεγιγνώσκετε (ξυγγιγνώσκω [takes the dative], have sympathy with) δήπου ἄν μοι, εἰ ἐν ἐκείνῃ τῇ φωνῇ 35 τε καὶ τῷ τρόπῳ ἔλεγον, ἐν οἷσπερ (ὅσπερ) ἐτεθράμμην, καὶ 36 δὴ καὶ νῦν τοῦτο ὑμῶν δέομαι δίκαιον (used adverbially), ὥς γέ μοι 37 δοκῶ τὸν μὲν τρόπον τῆς λέξεως (λέξις, εως, ἡ, style of speech) ἐᾶν (pres. inf. of ἐάω)·

Chapter XXIX

The Optative Mood
Crasis
Conjunctions

The Optative

<u>Form</u>

The present, future, aorist, perfect, and future perfect tenses (only the present and aorist in the New Testament) occur in the optative mood; but the future, perfect, and future perfect are very rare. Hence, only the present and aorist are considered in this grammar.

Present Optative of λύω

	Active		Middle and Passive	
	Singular	Plural	Singular	Plural
1.	λύοιμι	λύοιμεν	λυοίμην	λυοίμεθα
2.	λύοις	λύοιτε	λύοιο	λύοισθε
3.	λύοι	λύοιεν	λύοιτο	λύοιντο

Present Optative of δίδωμι

	Active		Middle and Passive	
	Singular	Plural	Singular	Plural
1.	διδοίην	διδοῖμεν	διδοίμην	διδοίμεθα
2.	διδοίης	διδοῖτε	διδοῖο	διδοῖσθε
3.	διδοίη	διδοῖεν	διδοῖτο	διδοῖντο

Present Optative of ἵστημι

	Active		Middle and Passive	
	Singular	Plural	Singular	Plural
1.	ἱσταίην	ἱσταῖμεν	ἱσταίμην	ἱσταίμεθα
2.	ἱσταίης	ἱσταῖτε	ἱσταῖο	ἱσταῖσθε
3.	ἱσταίη	ἱσταῖεν	ἱσταῖτο	ἱσταῖντο

Present Optative Conjugation of εἰμι

	Singular	Plural
1.	εἴην	εἴημεν or εἶμεν
2.	εἴης	εἴητε or εἶτε
3.	εἴη	εἴησαν or εἶεν

Present Optative of φιλέω

	Active		Middle and Passive	
	Singular	Plural	Singular	Plural
1.	φιλοίην	φιλοῖμεν	φιλοίμην	φιλοίμεθα
2.	φιλοίης	φιλοῖτε	φιλοῖο	φιλοῖσθε
3.	φιλοίη	φιλοῖεν	φιλοῖτο	φιλοῖντο

First Aorist Optative of λύω

	Active		Middle	
	Singular	Plural	Singular	Plural
1.	λύσαιμι	λύσαιμεν	λυσαίμην	λυσαίμεθα
2.	λύσαις or λύσειας	λύσαιτε	λύσαιο	λύσαισθε
3.	λύσαι or λύσειε	λύσαιεν or λύσειαν	λύσαιτο	λύσαιντο

Passive

	Singular	Plural
1.	λυθείην	λυθεῖμεν or λυθείημεν
2.	λυθείης	λυθεῖτε or λυθείητε
3.	λυθείη	λυθεῖεν or λυθείησαν

Second Aorist Optative of λαμβάνω

	Active		Middle	
	Singular	Plural	Singular	Plural
1.	λάβοιμι	λάβοιμεν	λαβοίμην	λαβοίμεθα
2.	λάβοις	λάβοιτε	λάβοιο	λάβοισθε
3.	λάβοι	λάβοιεν	λάβοιτο	λάβοιντο

Observe:
1. With some noticeable exceptions, the present and second aorist tenses use οι, and the first aorist uses αι.
2. All tenses have secondary endings.

Function

The optative is a potential mood, and the difference in tenses is a difference in kind of action. The significance of voice for the optative is the same as for the other moods. The optative is used in certain constructions and, just like the subjunctive, the particular construction determines how the optative will be translated. The New Testament has relatively few optatives since the subjunctive has largely replaced it.

The optative in independent clauses may express potentiality and wishes. The following are examples of the optative in wishes:

καὶ ἀποκριθεὶς εἶπεν αὐτῇ, Μηκέτι εἰς τὸν αἰῶνα ἐκ σοῦ μηδεὶς καρπὸν **φάγοι** (Mark 11:14): "And answering he said to it, '**May** no one ever **eat** fruit from you.'"

ἐπιμένωμεν τῇ ἁμαρτίᾳ, ἵνα ἡ χάρις πλεονάσῃ; μὴ **γένοιτο** (Romans 6:1-2); "Shall we continue in sin in order that grace may abound? **May** it not **happen**."

τεθναίην δίκην ἐπιθεὶς τῷ ἀδικοῦντι (The Apology XVI:31-32); "**May I die** after having placed vengeance upon the one who is doing wrong."

The optative with ἄν is used to express a future possibility. This potential optative is translated by "may," "might," "can," "would," or similar words.

Εὐξαίμην ἂν τῷ θεῷ ... σε ... γενέσθαι τοιούτους ὁποῖος καὶ ἐγώ εἰμι (Acts 26:29); "**I would pray** to God ... that you ... become such as even I myself am."

τὰ γὰρ ἀληθῆ, οἴομαι, οὐκ **ἂν ἐθέλοιεν** λέγειν (The Apology X:17-18); "For they **would** not, I think, **desire** to speak the truth."

The optative in dependent clauses in Classical Greek is characteristically used after secondary tenses; however, in the New Testament the subjunctive is used. No attempt is made in this grammar to discuss all of the various uses of the optative, and this is particularly true of the optative in dependent clauses.*

When the independent clause is in past time, the optative may be used with ἵνα, ὡς, or ὅπως to express purpose.

προσέταξαν ἀγαγεῖν ἐκ Σαλαμῖνος Λέοντα τὸν Σαλαμίνιον, **ἵνα ἀποθάνοι** (The Apology XX:21-23); "They ordered [them] to lead Leon the Salaminian out of Salamis **in order that** he **might die**."

---

* See p. 143 for the optative in less probable future conditional sentences.

The optative is used in indirect discourse and questions when the introductory verb is in past time.

ἀνεκρινάμην οὖν ἐμαυτῷ καὶ τῷ χρησμῷ, ὅτι μοι λυσιτελοῖ ὥσπερ ἔχω ἔχειν (The Apology VIII:16-17); "Therefore, I **answered** to myself and the oracle that it **was advantageous** for me to be just as I was."

ἤρετο γὰρ δή, εἴ τις ἐμοῦ εἴη σοφώτερος (The Apology V:33); "For he **was asking** if anyone **was** wiser than I."

διηπόρει ὁ Πέτρος τί ἂν εἴη τὸ ὅραμα ὃ εἶδεν (Acts 10:17); "Peter **was wondering** what the vision **was** which he had seen."

Crasis

Crasis is the contraction of a vowel or diphthong at the end of a word with a vowel or a diphthong beginning the following word: καὶ ἐκεῖνος becomes κἀκεῖνος (Luke 11:7). The hook above the contraction is called the coronis mark. In the New Testament καί and the article are the only words that contract with other words. The following examples illustrate crasis in the New Testament:

        τοὔνομα (Matt 27:57) for τὸ ὄνομα
        κἀγώ (John 1:31) for καὶ ἐγώ
        κἀμοί (Acts 10:38) for καὶ ἐμοί
        κἀμέ (John 16:32) for καὶ ἐμέ
        κἄν (Mark 5:28) for καὶ ἐάν
        κἀκεῖ (Mark 1:35) for καὶ ἐκεῖ
        κἀκεῖθεν (Mark 9:30) for καὶ ἐκεῖθεν

In Classical Greek, particularly in poetry, there is a greater variety of crasis than in the New Testament. The following words from *The Apology* illustrate this variety:

        τἀληθῆ (The Apology I:41) for τὰ ἀληθῆ
        τἄλλα (The Apology II:25) for τὰ ἄλλα
        κἄπειτα (The Apology VI:20) for καὶ ἔπειτα
        κἀγαθόν (The Apology VI:26) for καὶ ἀγαθόν
        ταὐτόν (The Apology VIII:7) for τὸ αὐτόν
        μεντἄν (The Apology XVIII:12) for μέντοι ἄν
        τοὐναντίον (The Apology XXIII:37) for τὸ ἐναντίον
        ἐγῷμαι (The Apology XXVII:32) for ἐγὼ οἶμαι.

Conjunctions

A conjunction connects words or groups of words. Coordinate conjunctions (καί, ἀλλά, δέ, ἤ, γάρ, οὖν, τε, διό, and ἄρα) connect words or groups of words that are independent of each other. Subordinate conjunctions (ὅτι, ἄχρι, ἐάν, εἰ, ἵνα, ὅπως, ὡς, and ἕως) connect a dependent clause to an independent clause.

Some conjunctions are used in pairs and correspond to English correlative conjunctions.

Τίς ἄρα οὗτός ἐστιν ὅτι **καὶ** ὁ ἄνεμος **καὶ** ἡ θάλασσα ὑπακούει αὐτῷ; (Mark 4:41); "What then is this that **both** the wind **and** the sea obey him?"

Τὸν μὲν πρῶτον λόγον ἐποιησάμην περὶ πάντων, . . . ὧν ἤρξατο ὁ Ἰησοῦς ποιεῖν **τε καὶ** διδάσκειν (Acts 1:1); "The first book I made concerning all things . . . which Jesus began **both** to do **and** to teach."

οὐδεὶς οἶδεν, **οὐδὲ** οἱ ἄγγελοι ἐν οὐρανῷ **οὐδὲ** ὁ υἱός (Mark 13:32); "No one knows, **neither** the angels in heaven **nor** the son."

Οὐδεὶς δύναται δυσὶ κυρίοις δουλεύειν· **ἢ** γὰρ τὸν ἕνα μισήσει καὶ τὸν ἕτερον ἀγαπήσει, **ἢ** ἑνὸς ἀνθέξεται καὶ τοῦ ἑτέρου καταφρονήσει (Matt. 6:24); "No one is able to serve two masters; for **either** he will hate the one and love the other, **or** he will be loyal to the one and despise the other."

μέν and δέ are often used to contrast words or ideas. "On the one hand . . . but on the other hand" clearly express the Greek meaning; however, this rather cumbersome translation is frequently replaced by "but." Observe these two translations of the same sentence.

τὸ **μὲν** πνεῦμα πρόθυμον ἡ **δὲ** σὰρξ ἀσθενής (Mark 14:38);
"**On the one hand** the spirit is willing, **but on the other hand** the flesh is weak."
"The spirit is willing, **but** the flesh is weak."

Vocabulary

1. ἀδικία, ας, ἡ	evil or injustice	
2. ἀκοή, ῆς, ἡ	report	(ἀκούω)
3. δένδρον, ου, τό	tree	(rhododendron)
4. ἐκεῖθεν, adverb	from there	
5. ἔλεος, ἐλέους, τό	mercy	
6. ἑορτή, ῆς, ἡ	feast	(heortology)
7. καθαρός, ά, όν	clean	(catharsis)
8. νεφέλη, ης, ἡ	cloud	(nephogram)

9. οὔπω, adverb — not yet
10. πνευματικός, ή, όν — spirital (pneumatic)
11. πόθεν
interrogative adverb — where
12. πορνεία, ας, ἡ — sexual immorality (pornography)
13. γαμέω, γαμήσω or γαμῶ, ἐγάμησα or ἔγημα, γεγάμηκα, γεγάμημαι, ἐγαμήθην, marry, (syngamy)
14. ἐλεέω, ἐλεήσω, ἠλέησα, ἠλέηκα, ἠλέημαι, ἠλεήθην, be merciful, (ἔλεος)
15. ἐλπίζω, ἐλπίσω or ἐλπιῶ, ἤλπισα, ἤλπικα, --, ἠλπίσθην, hope, (ἐλπίς)
16. ἐπικαλέω, ἐπικαλέσω, ἐπεκάλεσα, ἐπικέκληκα, ἐπικέκλημαι, ἐπεκλήθην, call or name, (καλέω)
17. καθαρίζω, καθαριῶ, ἐκαθάρισα, --, --, ἐκαθαρίσθην, cleanse, (catharize)
18. παραγγέλλω, παραγγελῶ, παρήγγειλα, παρήγγελκα, παρήγγελμαι, παρηγγέλθην, command, (ἄγγελος)
19. φιλέω, φιλήσω, ἐφίλησα, πεφίληκα, πεφίλημαι, ἐφιλήθην, love, (philogyny)
20. φωνέω, φωνήσω, ἐφώνησα, πεφώνηκα, πεφώνημαι, ἐφωνήθην, call (φωνή)

Translation
  Mark 4:24-29

The Apology I:37-II:8

37 ἴσως μὲν γὰρ 38 χείρων, ἴσως δὲ βελτίων (βελτίων, ον, genitive βελτίονος, comparative of ἀγαθός) ἂν εἴη· αὐτὸ δὲ τοῦτο 39 σκοπεῖν καὶ τούτῳ τὸν νοῦν προσέχειν, εἰ δίκαια 40 λέγω ἢ μή· δικαστοῦ μὲν γὰρ αὕτη ἀρετή, ῥήτορος 41 δὲ τἀληθῆ λέγειν.

II:1 Πρῶτον μὲν οὖν δίκαιός εἰμι ἀπολογήσασθαι, 2 ὦ ἄνδρες Ἀθηναῖοι, πρὸς τὰ πρῶτά μου 3 ψεύδη κατηγορημένα καὶ τοὺς πρώτους κατηγόρους, ἔπειτα δὲ πρὸς τὰ ὕστερα 5 καὶ τοὺς ὑστέρους. ἐμοῦ γὰρ πολλοὶ κατήγοροι 6 γεγόνασιν πρὸς ὑμᾶς καὶ πάλαι, πολλὰ ἤδη ἔτη καὶ 7 οὐδὲν ἀληθὲς λέγοντες, οὓς ἐγὼ μᾶλλον φοβοῦμαι ἢ 8 τοὺς ἀμφὶ (preposition with the accusative "around") Ἄνυτον (Ἄνυτος, ου, ὁ, Anytus) καίπερ ὄντας καὶ τούτους δεινούς.

Chapter XXX

Verbal Adjectives
Further Uses of the Cases

Verbal Adjectives

There are adjectives that are formed on verb roots but they are not participles. These adjectives do not have voice or tense and have as a suffix either τος or τεος.

Verbal adjectives ending with τεος indicate necessity. In Classical Greek they do not occur as often as adjectives ending with τος. Only one adjective, βλητέος, appears in the New Testament, and it is found once in Luke and once in a disputed text of Mark 2:22.

ἀλλὰ οἶνον νέον εἰς ἀσκοὺς καινοὺς **βλητέον** (Luke 5:38); "But new wine **must be put** into fresh wineskins."

ὅμως τοῦτο μὲν ἴτω ὅπῃ τῷ θεῷ φίλον, τῷ δὲ νόμῳ **πειστέον**, καὶ **ἀπολογητέον** (The Apology II:44-45); "Nevertheless let this go in a way pleasing to God, but **it is necessary to obey** the law and **defense must be made**."

Verbal adjectives with the suffix τος are common in Classical and New Testament Greek.

εἶ ὁ υἱός μου ὁ **ἀγαπητός** (Mark 1:11); "You are my **beloved** son."

ἐμοὶ γὰρ δοκεῖ οὑτοσί . . . εἶναι . . . **ἀκόλαστος** (The Apology XIV:35-37); "For this man seems to me . . . to be . . . **unrestrained**."

Further Uses of the Cases

Each of the five cases has one or more basic significance, and the basic significances have various uses. Some grammarians classify the cases according to basic significances; hence, they say that there are eight cases. Whether a grammarian classifies the cases according to spelling (five case system) or to significance makes little or no difference in reaching the objective of an accurate translation.* In the following chart no attempt is made to list all of the uses of the cases.

Five Case Classification	Basic Significance	Use	Eight Case Classification
Nominative	Designation	subject, predicate complement	Nominative
Genitive	Description	absolute, objective & subjective, partitive, possession, price, quality, source, time, with verbs of sensation & accusing	Genitive
	Separation	separation, comparison	Ablative
Dative	Interest	advantage, indirect object, possession	Dative
	Location	place, time	Locative
	Instrument	association, means, measure of difference	Instrumental
Accusative	Limitation	double & predicate, extent, object, reference, subject of infinitive	Accusative
Vocative	Address		Vocative

The uses of the cases that are illustrated in the following discussion are listed in the preceding chart but have not been discussed previously in this grammar.

Genitives of Content, Price, Quality, and Source

The genitive may describe from the standpoint of content, price, quality, or source.

---

* Some grammarians put much emphasis on the differences between κοινή and Attic Greek: the disappearance of dual number, the disuse of the optative mood, the frequent use of periphrastics, and the various changes of syntax and spelling. In translating, however, a student has little trouble with these differences if he has a basic knowledge of either κοινή or Attic grammar.

πεπληρώκατε τὴν Ἰερουσαλὴμ τῆς **διδαχῆς** ὑμῶν (Acts 5:28); "You have filled Jerusalem **with** your **teaching**."

ἀγοράσωμεν **δηναρίων διακοσίων** ἄρτους; (Mark 5:37); "Shall we buy bread **worth two hundred denarii**."

ἐγένετο Ἰωάννης . . . κηρύσσων βάπτισμα **μετανοίας** (Mark 1:4); "John came . . . preaching a baptism **of repentance**."

ἦν ὁ Ἰωάννης ἐνδεδυμένος τρίχας **καμήλου** (Mark 1:6); "John wore hair **from a camel**."

Objective and Subjective Genitives

The genitive is used with nouns of action: ἀγάπη, γραφή, δῶρον, ἔργον, πίστις, and others. If the substantive in the genitive receives the action which is expressed in the noun of action, it is called an objective genitive.

> ὁ Ἰησοῦς λέγει αὐτοῖς, Εἰ ἔχετε πίστιν **θεοῦ** (Mark 11:22); "Jesus said to them, 'If you have faith **in God**.'"

If the substantive in the genitive does the action, it is a subjective genitive.

> ἰδὼν ὁ Ἰησοῦς τὴν πίστιν **αὐτῶν** λέγει τῷ παραλυτικῷ, Τέκνον, ἀφίενται σου αἱ ἁμαρτίαι (Mark 2:5); "Having seen **their** faith, Jesus said to the paralytic, 'Son, **your** sins are forgiven.'"

The context, not the genitive substantive or the noun of action, determines whether the genitive is objective or subjective. In the above illustrations the noun of action πίστις is followed once by the objective genitive and once by the subjective genitive.

Partitive Genitive

The genitive may denote a whole, a part of which is denoted by the noun it limits.

> Ὅ τι ἐάν με αἰτήσῃς δώσω σοι ἕως ἡμίσους τῆς **βασιλείας** μου (Mark 6:23); "'Whatever you ask me, I shall give you up to half **of** my **kingdom**.'"

Genitive of Separation

Without a preposition this genitive most often follows verbs of departure, ceasing, lacking, or related ideas.

> οὐκ ἀφίστατο τοῦ **ἱεροῦ** (Luke 2:37); "She did not leave the **temple**."

Dative of Possession
The basic significance of interest for the dative can be strong enough to show possession.

οὐκ ἔστι **σοι** μερίς (Acts 8:21); "It is not **your** portion."

Dative of Association
The dative is used with words denoting association.

ἀφέντες τὰ δίκτυα ἠκολούθησαν **αὐτῷ** (Mark 1:18): "After having left their nets, they followed **him**."

Dative of Measure of Difference
With comparatives the dative is used to express the degree or measure of difference.

ἔοικα γοῦν τούτου γε **σμικρῷ** . . . σοφώτερος εἶναι (The Apology VI:27-29); "Therefore, I seem to be wiser **to a small degree** . . . than this man."

ὁ δὲ **πολλῷ** μᾶλλον ἔκραζεν (Mark 10:48); "But he was crying out more **by much**."

Double Accusative
Verbs of asking, teaching, clothing, and similar verbs often have two accusatives, one of the person and one of the thing.

ἤρξατο διδάσκειν **αὐτοὺς πολλά** (Mark 6:34); "He began to teach **them many things**."

ἐνέδυσαν **αὐτὸν τὰ ἱμάτια τὰ ἴδια** (Mark 15:20); "They dressed **him with his own garments**."

Predicate Accusative
Verbs of choosing, naming, calling, and other similar verbs often take two accusatives; the second accusative is the predicate accusative which is practically in apposition with the first (the direct object).

πεποιήκατε **αὐτὸν σπήλαιον** λῃστῶν (Mark 11:17); "You have made it a **den** of robbers."

μάρτυρας δὲ αὐτοὺς ὑμῶν τοὺς **πολλοὺς** παρέχομαι (The Apology III:19-20); "And I offer the **many** of you yourselves **as witnesses**."

Accusative of Reference

The accusative may denote that with reference to which some statement is true.

εἴχομεν ἄν αὐτοῖν ἐπιστάτην λαβεῖν καὶ μισθώσασθαι, ὅς ἔμελλεν αὐτὼ καλώ τε κἀγαθὼ ποιήσει τὴν προσήκουσαν **ἀρετήν** (The Apology IV:19-20); "We would have been able to secure and to hire an overseer for them, who would make them both fine and good **with reference to the virtue which is fitting**."

πάντα ἐγκρατεύεται (I Cor. 9:25); "He is exercising self-control **with reference to all things**."

Vocabulary

1. ἄπιστος, ον — unfaithful (πιστός)
2. ἀστήρ, ἀστέρος, ὁ — star (astronaut)
3. διότι, conjunction — because
4. ἐκλεκτός, ή, όν — elect (eclecticism)
5. ἐπιστολή, ῆς, ἡ — letter (epistle)
6. λευκός, ή, όν — white (leukemia)
7. νέος, α, ον — new (neophite)
8. νοῦς, νοός, ὁ — mind (noetic)
9. παῖς, παιδός, ἡ or ὁ — child (pedagogue)
10. παρουσία, ας, ἡ — coming or presence (Parousia)
11. πόσος, η, ον — how much (posology)
12. σωτήρ, σωτῆρος, ὁ — Savior (soteriology)
13. ἐνδύω, ἐνδύσω, ἐνέδυσα or ἐνέδυν, ἐνδέδυκα, ἐνδέδυμαι, ἐνεδύθην, dress
14. ἥκω, ἥξω, ἧξα, ἧκα, --, --, come or have come
15. νικάω, νικήσω, ἐνίκησα, νενίκηκα, νενίκημαι, ἐνικήθην, conquer, (Nicholas)
16. προφητεύω, --, ἐπροφήτευσα, --, --, --, proclaim a divine message, (προφήτης)
17. σκανδαλίζω, --, ἐσκανδάλισα, --, --, ἐσκανδαλίσθην, offend, (scandalize)
18. τελέω, τελῶ, ἐτέλεσα, τετέλεκα, τετέλεσμαι, ἐτελέσθην, finish, (teleology)
19. φαίνω, φανῶ, ἔφηνα, πέφηνα, πέφασμαι, ἐφάνην, shine or appear, (phenomenon)
20. φεύγω, φεύξομαι, ἔφυγον, πέφευγα, πέφυγμαι, --, flee, (fugue)

Translation
Mark 4:30-34

The Apology II:9-22
9 ἀλλὰ ἐκεῖνοι δεινότεροι, ὦ ἄνδρες, οἳ ὑμῶν τοὺς 10 πολλοὺς ἐκ παίδων παραλαμβάνοντες ἔπειθόν τε καὶ 11 κατηγόρουν ἐμοῦ μᾶλλον οὐδὲν ἀληθές, ὡς ἔστιν τις 12 Σωκράτης (Σωκράτης, ους, ὁ, Socrates), σοφὸς ἀνήρ, τά τε μετέωρα (μετεώρος, on, in the air) φροντιστὴς (φροντιστής, οῦ, ὁ speculator) 13 καὶ τὰ ὑπὸ γῆς ἅπαντα ἀνεζητηκὼς καὶ τὸν ἥττω (ἥττων, ον, comparative adjective, weaker) 14 λόγον κρείττω ποιῶν. οὗτοι, ὦ ἄνδρες Ἀθηναῖοι, οἱ 15 ταύτην τὴν φήμην κατασκεδάσαντες (κατασκεδάννυμι, spread abroad), οἱ δεινοί εἰσίν 16 μου κατήγοροι· οἱ γὰρ ἀκούοντες ἡγοῦνται τοὺς 17 ταῦτα ζητοῦντας οὐδὲ θεοὺς νομίζειν. ἔπειτά εἰσιν 18 οὗτοι οἱ κατήγοροι πολλοὶ καὶ πολὺν χρόνον ἤδη 19 κατηγορηκότες, ἔτι δὲ καὶ ἐν ταύτῃ τῇ ἡλικίᾳ 20 λέγοντες πρὸς ὑμᾶς ἐν ᾗ ἂν μάλιστα ἐπιστεύσατε, 21 παῖδες ὄντες ἔνιοι (ἔνιοι, αι, α, plural adjective, some) δ' ὑμῶν καὶ μειράκια (μειράκιον, ου, τό, lad), ἀτεχνῶς (adverb, literally) 22 ἐρήμην κατηγοροῦντες ἀπολογουμένου οὐδενός.

Luke 18:7
ὁ δὲ θεὸς οὐ μὴ ποιήσῃ τὴν ἐκδίκησιν τῶν ἐκλεκτῶν αὐτοῦ τῶν βοώντων αὐτῷ ἡμέρας καὶ νυκτός.
Acts 4:8-9
τότε Πέτρος πλησθεὶς πνεύματος ἁγίου εἶπεν πρὸς αὐτούς, Ἄρχοντες τοῦ λαοῦ καὶ πρεσβύτεροι, εἰ ἡμεῖς σήμερον ἀνακρινόμεθα ἐπὶ εὐεργεσίᾳ ἀνθρώπου ἀσθενοῦς, ἐν τίνι οὗτος σέσωται.
Acts 5:8
ἀπεκρίθη δὲ πρὸς αὐτὴν Πέτρος, Εἰπέ μοι, εἰ τοσούτου τὸ χωρίον ἀπέδοσθε; ἡ δὲ εἶπεν, Ναί, τοσούτου.
Eph. 4:15
ἀληθεύοντες δὲ ἐν ἀγάπῃ αὐξήσωμεν εἰς αὐτὸν τὰ πάντα, ὅς ἐστιν ἡ κεφαλή, Χριστός.
The Apology V:13-14
τῷ ὄντι γὰρ κινδυνεύω ταύτην εἶναι σοφός.

CONTENTS OF APPENDIX

Paradigm		Page
I	ἀγαθός	165
II	πᾶς	166
III	ἔθνος	166
IV	πόλις	167
V	λύω	168
VI	ἵστημι	170
VII	εἰμί	171
VIII	εἶμι	171
IX	ζάω	171
X	κάθημαι	172
XI	τιμάω	172
XII	δηλόω	174
XIII	φημί	175
XIV	Dual of ἀγαθός and ὁ	175
XV	οἶδα	176
XVI	ἡδύς	176
XVII	Third Person Personal Pronoun	177
XVIII	Dual of πόλις and ἔθνος	177
XIX	ἀλήθεια	177

Appendix

The majority of beginning Greek grammars use the appendix to summarize the paradigms presented in the main body of the text. That is not the intent of this appendix. Rather its purpose is to give a small number of paradigms which may be the means of a rapid reviewing of the bulk of the forms encountered in elementary Greek. This appendix also contains a few forms, such as duals, that will be particularly helpful in other Greek courses.

I.   ἀγαθός

	Singular		
	Masculine	Feminine	Neuter
Nom.	ἀγαθός	ἀγαθή	ἀγαθόν
Gen.	ἀγαθοῦ	ἀγαθῆς	ἀγαθοῦ
Dat.	ἀγαθῷ	ἀγαθῇ	ἀγαθῷ
Acc.	ἀγαθόν	ἀγαθήν	ἀγαθόν
Voc.	ἀγαθέ	ἀγαθή	ἀγαθόν

	Plural		
	Masculine	Feminine	Neuter
Nom.	ἀγαθοί	ἀγαθαί	ἀγαθά
Gen.	ἀγαθῶν	ἀγαθῶν	ἀγαθῶν
Dat.	ἀγαθοῖς	ἀγαθαῖς	ἀγαθοῖς
Acc.	ἀγαθούς	ἀγαθάς	ἀγαθά
Nom.	ἀγαθοί	ἀγαθαί	ἀγαθά

When the student reviews ἀγαθός, he reviews the declensions of adjectives following the first and second declensions, first and second declension nouns, the definite article ὁ, the demonstrative pronouns (οὗτος, ἐκεῖνος, and ὅδε), the relative pronoun ὅς, the third person personal pronoun αὐτός, the reflexive pronoun ἐμαυτοῦ, the reciprocal pronoun ἀλλήλων, and middle and passive participles (excluding masculine and neuter aorist passive participles). Thus with the exception of the declension of ἐγώ and σύ (Chapter X), a study of ἀγαθός is a review of the declensions of the first semester of Greek.

II.   πᾶς

	Masculine	Singular Feminine	Neuter
Nom.	πᾶς	πᾶσα	πᾶν
Gen.	παντός	πάσης	παντός
Dat.	παντί	πάσῃ	παντί
Acc.	πάντα	πᾶσαν	πᾶν
		Plural	
Nom.	πάντες	πᾶσαι	πάντα
Gen.	πάντων	πασῶν	πάντων
Dat.	πᾶσι (ν)	πάσαις	πᾶσι (ν)
Acc.	πάντας	πάσας	πάντα

When studying πᾶς, a student is reviewing the declension of other adjectives that follow the third declension, third declension nouns, certain cardinal numbers (εἷς, τρεῖς, and τέσσαρες), the indefinite pronoun τις, the interrogative pronoun τίς, and masculine and neuter active participles (along with the masculine and neuter passive participles). If a student wishes to review the declensions of the second semester, in addition to πᾶς he should go over the declensions of ἔθνος and πόλις (Chapter XVII). They are third declension nouns; but because of obvious peculiarities and the large number of nouns that have the same peculiarities, it is advantageous to give them special attention.

III.   ἔθνος

	Singular	Plural
N., A., V.	ἔθνος	ἔθνη
Gen.	ἔθνους	ἐθνῶν
Dat.	ἔθνει	ἔθνεσι (ν)

IV.   πόλις

	Singular	Plural
Nom.	πόλις	πόλεις
Gen.	πόλεως	πόλεων
Dat.	πόλει	πόλεσι (ν)
Acc.	πόλιν	πόλεις
Voc.	πόλι	πόλεις

In order to complete a review of a large part of the inflection of first year Greek, the student should study the conjugations of λύω, εἰμι, and ἵστημι.

v.

λύω

		λύω Active		λύσω Active	ἔλυσα Active		λέλυκα Active		λέλυμαι		ἐλύθην	
		Present	Imperfect	Future	Aorist		Perfect	Pluperfect	Perfect	Pluperfect	Aorist	Future
IND												
S	1	λύω	ἔλυον	λύσω	ἔλυσα		λέλυκα	ἐλελύκειν				
	2	λύεις	ἔλυες	λύσεις	ἔλυσας		λέλυκας	ἐλελύκεις				
	3	λύει	ἔλυε (ν)	λύσει	ἔλυσε (ν)		λέλυκε (ν)	ἐλελύκει				
P	1	λύομεν	ἐλύομεν	λύσομεν	ἐλύσαμεν		λελύκαμεν	ἐλελύκειμεν				
	2	λύετε	ἐλύετε	λύσετε	ἐλύσατε		λελύκατε	ἐλελύκειτε				
	3	λύουσι (ν)	ἔλυον	λύσουσι	ἔλυσαν		λελύκασι	ἐλελύκεισαν				
SUBJ												
S	1	λύω			λύσω		λελύκω					
	2	λύῃς			λύσῃς		λελύκῃς					
	3	λύῃ			λύσῃ		λελύκῃ					
P	1	λύωμεν			λύσωμεν		λελύκωμεν					
	2	λύητε			λύσητε		λελύκητε					
	3	λύωσι (ν)			λύσωσι (ν)		λελύκωσι (ν)					
IMPV												
S	2	λῦε			λῦσον		λελυκὼς ἴσθι					
	3	λυέτω			λυσάτω		λελυκὼς ἔστω					
P	2	λύετε			λύσατε		λελυκότες ἔστε					
	3	λυέτωσαν			λυσάτωσαν		λελυκότες ἔστων					
OPT												
S	1	λύοιμι		λύσοιμι	λύσαιμι		λελύκοιμι					
	2	λύοις		λύσοις	λύσαις		λελύκοις					
	3	λύοι		λύσοι	λύσαι		λελύκοι					
P	1	λύοιμεν		λύσοιμεν	λύσαιμεν		λελύκοιμεν					
	2	λύοιτε		λύσοιτε	λύσαιτε		λελύκοιτε					
	3	λύοιεν		λύσοιεν	λύσαιεν		λελύκοιεν					
INF		λύειν		λύσειν	λῦσαι		λελυκέναι					
PART		λύων (λύοντος)		λύσων	λύσας		λελυκώς (λελυκότος)					
		λύουσα (λυούσης)		λύσουσα	λύσασα		λελυκυῖα (λελυκυίας)					
		λῦον (λύοντος)		λῦσον	λῦσαν		λελυκός (λελυκότος)					

	Present	Imperfect	Future	Aorist	Perfect	Pluperfect	Aorist Passive	Future Passive
S 1	λύομαι	ἐλυόμην	λύσομαι	ἐλυσάμην	λέλυμαι	ἐλελύμην	ἐλύθην	λυθήσομαι
S 2	λύῃ, ει	ἐλύου	λύσῃ, ει	ἐλύσω	λέλυσαι	ἐλέλυσο	ἐλύθης	λυθήσῃ, ει
S 3	λύεται	ἐλύετο	λύσεται	ἐλύσατο	λέλυται	ἐλέλυτο	ἐλύθη	λυθήσεται
P 1	λυόμεθα	ἐλυόμεθα	λυσόμεθα	ἐλυσάμεθα	λελύμεθα	ἐλελύμεθα	ἐλύθημεν	λυθησόμεθα
P 2	λύεσθε	ἐλύεσθε	λύσεσθε	ἐλύσασθε	λέλυσθε	ἐλέλυσθε	ἐλύθητε	λυθήσεσθε
P 3	λύονται	ἐλύοντο	λύσονται	ἐλύσαντο	λέλυνται	ἐλέλυντο	ἐλύθησαν	λυθήσονται
SUBJ								
S 1	λύωμαι			λύσωμαι	λελυμένος ὦ		λυθῶ	
S 2	λύῃ			λύσῃ	λελυμένος ᾖς		λυθῇς	
S 3	λύηται			λύσηται	λελυμένος ᾖ		λυθῇ	
P 1	λυώμεθα			λυσώμεθα	λελυμένοι ὦμεν		λυθῶμεν	
P 2	λύησθε			λύσησθε	λελυμένοι ἦτε		λυθῆτε	
P 3	λύωνται			λύσωνται	λελυμένοι ὦσι		λυθῶσι	
IMPV								
S 2	λύου			λῦσαι	λέλυσο		λύθητι	
S 3	λυέσθω			λυσάσθω	λελύσθω		λυθήτω	
P 2	λύεσθε			λύσασθε	λέλυσθε		λύθητε	
P 3	λυέσθωσαν			λυσάσθων	λελύσθων		λυθήτωσαν	
OPT								
S 1	λυοίμην		λυσοίμην	λυσαίμην	λελυμένος εἴην		λυθείην	λυθησοίμην
S 2	λύοιο		λύσοιο	λύσαιο	λελυμένος εἴης		λυθείης	λυθήσοιο
S 3	λύοιτο		λύσοιτο	λύσαιτο	λελυμένος εἴη		λυθείη	λυθήσοιτο
P 1	λυοίμεθα		λυσοίμεθα	λυσαίμεθα	λελυμένοι εἴημεν, εἶμεν		λυθείημεν	λυθησοίμεθα
P 2	λύοισθε		λύσοισθε	λύσαισθε	λελυμένοι εἴητε, εἶτε		λυθείητε	λυθήσοισθε
P 3	λύοιντο		λύσοιντο	λύσαιντο	λελυμένοι εἴησαν, εἶεν		λυθείησαν	λυθήσοιντο
INF	λύεσθαι		λύσεσθαι	λύσασθαι	λελύσθαι		λυθῆναι	λυθήσεσθαι
PART	λυόμενος, ου		λυσόμενος	λυσάμενος	λελυμένος		λυθείς	λυθησόμενος
	λυομένη		λυσομένη	λυσαμένη	λελυμένη		λυθεῖσα	λυθησομένη
	λυόμενον, ου		λυσόμενον	λυσάμενον	λελυμένον		λυθέν	λυθησόμενον
							λυθέντος	

VI.

ἵστημι

		Active Present	Imperfect	MID & PASS Present	Imperfect	Active Second Aorist
IND						
S	1	ἵστημι	ἵστην	ἵσταμαι	ἱστάμην	ἔστην
S	2	ἵστης	ἵστης	ἵστασαι	ἵστασο	ἔστης
S	3	ἵστησι(ν)	ἵστη	ἵσταται	ἵστατο	ἔστη
P	1	ἵσταμεν	ἵσταμεν	ἱστάμεθα	ἱστάμεθα	ἔστημεν
P	2	ἵστατε	ἵστατε	ἵστασθε	ἵστασθε	ἔστητε
P	3	ἱστᾶσι(ν)	ἵστασαν	ἵστανται	ἵσταντο	ἔστησαν
SUBJ						
S	1	ἱστῶ		ἱστῶμαι		στῶ
S	2	ἱστῇς		ἱστῇ		στῇς
S	3	ἱστῇ		ἱστῆται		στῇ
P	1	ἱστῶμεν		ἱστώμεθα		στῶμεν
P	2	ἱστῆτε		ἱστῆσθε		στῆτε
P	3	ἱστῶσι(ν)		ἱστῶνται		στῶσι(ν)
IMPV						
S	2	ἵστη		ἵστασο		στῆθι
S	3	ἱστάτω		ἱστάσθω		στήτω
P	2	ἵστατε		ἵστασθε		στῆτε
P	3	ἱστάντων		ἱστάσθων		στάντων
OPT						
S	1	ἱσταίην		ἱσταίμην		σταίην
S	2	ἱσταίης		ἱσταῖο		σταίης
S	3	ἱσταίη		ἱσταῖτο		σταίη
P	1	ἱσταῖμεν / ἱσταίημεν		ἱσταίμεθα		σταῖμεν / σταίημεν
P	2	ἱσταῖτε / ἱσταίητε		ἱσταῖσθε		σταῖτε / σταίητε
P	3	ἱσταῖεν / ἱσταίησαν		ἱσταῖντο		σταῖεν / σταίησαν
INF		ἱστάναι		ἵστασθαι		στῆναι
PART		ἱστάς, ἱστάντος ἱστᾶσα, ἱστάσης ἱστάν, ἱστάντος		ἱστάμενος-α-ον		στάς, στάντος στᾶσα, στάσης στάν, στάντος

There is no second aorist middle of ἵστημι. Except for the first principle part and the second aorist of the third principle part, ἵστημι is the same as the ω conjugation.

VII. εἰμί

		Present				Imperfect	Future	
		IND	SUBJ	OPT	IMPV	IND	IND	OPT
S	1	εἰμί	ὦ	εἴην		ἤμην	ἔσομαι	ἐσοίμην
	2	εἶ	ᾖς	εἴης	ἴσθι	ἦς	ἔσῃ	ἔσοιο
	3	ἐστί (ν)	ᾖ	εἴη	ἔστω	ἦν	ἔσται	ἔσοιτο
P	1	ἐσμέν	ὦμεν	εἶμεν or εἴημεν		ἦμεν	ἐσόμεθα	ἐσοίμεθα
	2	ἐστέ	ἦτε	εἶτε or εἴητε	ἔστε	ἦτε	ἔσεσθε	ἔσοισθε
	3	εἰσί (ν)	ὦσι (ν)	εἶεν or εἴησαν	ἔστωσαν	ἦσαν	ἔσονται	ἔσοιντο

INF εἶναι   ἔσεσθαι

PART ὤν, ὄντος   ἐσόμενος, η, ον
 οὖσα, οὔσης
 ὄν, ὄντος

VIII. εἶμι

		Present				Imperfect
		IND	SUBJ	OPT	IMPV	IND
S	1	εἶμι	ἴω	ἴοιμι or ἰοίην		ᾖα or ᾔειν
	2	εἶ	ἴῃς	ἴοις	ἴθι	ᾔεισθα or ᾔεις
	3	εἶσι	ἴῃ	ἴοι	ἴτω	ᾔειν or ᾔει
D	2	ἴτον	ἴητον	ἴοιτον	ἴτον	ᾖτον
	3	ἴτον	ἴητον	ἴοιτον	ἴτων	ᾔτην
P	1	ἴμεν	ἴωμεν	ἴοιμεν		ᾖμεν
	2	ἴτε	ἴητε	ἴοιτε	ἴτε	ᾖτε
	3	ἴασι	ἴωσι	ἴοιεν	ἰόντων	ᾖσαν or ᾔεσαν

INF ἰέναι

PART ἰών, ἰόντος
 ἰοῦσα, ἰούσης
 ἰόν, ἰόντος

IX. ζάω

		Present		Imperfect
		IND and SUBJ	IMPV	IND
S	1	ζῶ		ἔζων
	2	ζῇς	ζῆ	ἔζης
	3	ζῇ	ζήτω	ἔζη
D	2	ζῆτον	ζῆτον	ἐζῆτον
	3	ζῆτον	ζήτων	ἐζήτην

P	1	ζῶμεν		ἐζῶμεν
	2	ζῆτε	ζῆτε	ἐζῆτε
	3	ζῶσι (ν)	ζώντων	ἔζων

INF ζῆν   PART ζῶν, ζῶσα, ζῶν

X.   κάθημαι

IND		Present		Imperfect
S	1	κάθημαι		ἐκαθήμην
	2	κάθησαι		ἐκάθησο
	3	κάθηται		ἐκάθητο
D	2	κάθησθον		ἐκάθησθον
	3	κάθησθον		ἐκαθήσθην
P	1	καθήμεθα		ἐκαθήμεθα
	2	κάθησθε		ἐκάθησθε
	3	κάθηνται		ἐκάθηντο

		SUBJ	IMPV	OPT
S	1	καθῶμαι		καθοίμην
	2	καθῇ	κάθησο	καθοῖο
	3	καθῆται	καθήσθω	καθοῖτο
D	2	καθῆσθον	κάθησθον	καθοῖσθον
	3	καθῆσθον	καθήσθων	καθοίσθην
P	1	καθώμεθα		καθοίμεθα
	2	καθῆσθε	κάθησθε	καθοῖσθε
	3	καθῶνται	καθήσθων	καθοῖντο

INF καθῆσθαι   PART καθήμενος, η, ον

XI.   τιμάω
Present

IND		Active		Middle and Passive	
S	1	τιμῶ	(τιμάω)	τιμῶμαι	(τιμάομαι)
	2	τιμᾷς	(τιμάεις)	τιμᾷ	(τιμάῃ, -άει)
	3	τιμᾷ	(τιμάει)	τιμᾶται	(τιμάεται)
D	2	τιμᾶτον	(τιμάετον)	τιμᾶσθον	(τιμάεσθον)
	3	τιμᾶτον	(τιμάετον)	τιμᾶσθον	(τιμάεσθον)
P	1	τιμῶμεν	(τιμάομεν)	τιμώμεθα	(τιμαόμεθα)
	2	τιμᾶτε	(τιμάετε)	τιμᾶσθε	(τιμάεσθε)
	3	τιμῶσι (ν)	(τιμάουσι)	τιμῶνται	(τιμάονται)

SUBJ

S	1	τιμῶ	(τιμάω)	τιμῶμαι	(τιμάωμαι)
	2	τιμᾷς	(τιμάῃς)	τιμᾷ	(τιμάῃ)
	3	τιμᾷ	(τιμάῃ)	τιμᾶται	(τιμάηται)
D	2	τιμᾶτον	(τιμάητον)	τιμᾶσθον	(τιμάησθον)
	3	τιμᾶτον	(τιμάητον)	τιμᾶσθον	(τιμάησθον)
P	1	τιμῶμεν	(τιμάωμεν)	τιμώμεθα	(τιμαώμεθα)
	2	τιμᾶτε	(τιμάητε)	τιμᾶσθε	(τιμάησθε)
	3	τιμῶσι (ν)	(τιμάωσι)	τιμῶνται	(τιμάωνται)

IMPV

S	2	τίμα	(τίμαε)	τιμῶ	(τιμάου)
	3	τιμάτω	(τιμαέτω)	τιμάσθω	(τιμαέσθω)
D	2	τιμῶτον	(τιμάετον)	τιμᾶσθον	(τιμάεσθον)
	3	τιμάτων	(τιμαέτων)	τιμάσθων	(τιμαέσθων)
P	2	τιμᾶτε	(τιμάετε)	τιμᾶσθε	(τιμάεσθε)
	3	τιμώντων	(τιμαόντων)	τιμάσθων	(τιμαέσθων)

OPT

S	1	τιμῷην	(τιμαοίην)	τιμῴμην	(τιμαοίμην)
	2	τιμῴης	(τιμαοίης)	τιμῷο	(τιμάοιο)
	3	τιμῴη	(τιμαοία)	τιμῷτο	(τιμάοιτο)
D	2	τιμῷτον	(τιμάοιτον)	τιμῷσθον	(τιμάοισθον)
	3	τιμῴτην	(τιμαοίην)	τιμῴσθην	(τιμαοίσθην)
P	1	τιμῷμεν	(τιμάοιμεν)	τιμῴμεθα	(τιμαοίμεθα)
	2	τιμῷτε	(τιμάοιτε)	τιμῷσθε	(τιμάοισθε)
	3	τιμῷεν	(τιμάοιεν)	τιμῷντο	(τιμάοιντο)

Imperfect

Active			Middle and Passive	

S	1	ἐτίμων	(ἐτίμαον)	ἐτιμώμην	(ἐτιμαόμην)
	2	ἐτίμας	(ἐτίμαες)	ἐτιμῶ	(ἐτιμάου)
	3	ἐτίμα	(ετίμαε)	ἐτιμᾶτο	(ἐτιμάετο)
D	2	ἐτιμᾶτον	(ἐτιμάετον)	ἐτιμᾶσθον	(ἐτιμάεσθον)
	3	ἐτιμάτην	(ἐτιμαέτην)	ἐτιμάσθην	(ἐτιμαέσθην)
P	1	ἐτιμῶμεν	(ἐτιμάομεν)	ἐτιμώμεθα	(ἐτιμαόμεθα)
	2	ἐτιμᾶτε	(ἐτιμάετε)	ἐτιμᾶσθε	(ἐτιμάεσθε)
	3	ἐτίμων	(ἐτίμαον)	ἐτιμῶντο	(ἐτιμάοντο)

PRES INF τιμᾶν (τιμάειν) τιμᾶσθαι (τιμάεσθαι)

PRES PART τιμῶν (τιμάων) τιμώμενος (τιμαόμενος)

XII. δηλόω
Present

		Active		Middle and Passive	
IND					
S	1	δηλῶ	(δηλόω)	δηλοῦμαι	(δηλόομαι)
	2	δηλοῖς	(δηλόεις)	δηλοῖ	(δηλόῃ, -όει)
	3	δηλοῖ	(δηλόει)	δηλοῦται	(δηλόεται)
D	2	δηλοῦτον	(δηλόετον)	δηλοῦσθον	(δηλόεσθον)
	3	δηλοῦτον	(δηλόετον)	δηλοῦσθον	(δηλόεσθον)
	1	δηλοῦμεν	(δηλόομεν)	δηλούμεθα	(δηλοόμεθα)
P	2	δηλοῦτε	(δηλόετε)	δηλοῦσθε	(δηλόεσθε)
	3	δηλοῦσι (ν)	(δηλόουσι)	δηλοῦνται	(δηλόονται)
SUBJ					
S	1	δηλῶ	(δηλόω)	δηλῶμαι	(δηλόωμαι)
	2	δηλοῖς	(δηλόῃς)	δηλοῖ	(δηλόῃ)
	3	δηλοῖ	(δηλόῃ)	δηλῶται	(δηλόηται)
D	2	δηλῶτον	(δηλόητον)	δηλῶσθον	(δηλόησθων)
	3	δηλῶτον	(δηλόητον)	δηλῶσθον	(δηλόησθον)
	1	δηλῶμεν	(δηλόωμεν)	δηλώμεθα	(δηλοώμεθα)
P	2	δηλῶτε	(δηλόητε)	δηλῶσθε	(δηλόησθε)
	3	δηλῶσι (ν)	(δηλόωσι)	δηλῶνται	(δηλόωνται)
IMPV					
S	2	δήλου	(δήλοε)	δηλοῦ	(δηλόου)
	3	δηλούτω	(δηλοέτω)	δηλούσθω	(δηλοέσθω)
D	2	δηλοῦτον	(δηλόετον)	δηλοῦσθον	(δηλόεσθον)
	3	δηλούτων	(δηλοέτων)	δηλούσθων	(δηλοέσθων)
P	2	δηλοῦτε	(δηλόετε)	δηλοῦσθε	(δηλόεσθε)
	3	δηλούντων	(δηλοόντων)	δηλούσθων	(δηλοέσθων)
OPT					
	1	δηλοίην	(δηλοοίην)	δηλοίμην	(δηλοοίμην)
S	2	δηλοίης	(δηλοοίης)	δηλοῖο	(δηλόοιο)
	3	δηλοίη	(δηλοοίη)	δηλοῖτο	(δηλόοιτο)
D	2	δηλοῖτον	(δηλόοιτον)	δηλοῖσθον	(δηλόοισθον)
	3	δηλοίτην	(δηλοοίτην)	δηλοίσθην	(δηλοοίσθην)
	1	δηλοῖμεν	(δηλόοιμεν)	δηλοίμεθα	(δηλοοίμεθα)
P	2	δηλοῖτε	(δηλόοιτε)	δηλοῖσθε	(δηλόοισθε)
	3	δηλοῖεν	(δηλόοιεν)	δηλοῖντο	(δηλόοιντο)

Imperfect

IND		Active		Middle and Passive	
S	1	ἐδήλουν	(ἐδήλοον)	ἐδηλούμην	(ἐδηλοόμην)
	2	ἐδήλους	(ἐδήλοες)	ἐδηλοῦ	(ἐδηλόου)
	3	ἐδήλου	(ἐδήλοε)	ἐδηλοῦτο	(ἐδηλόετο)
D	2	ἐδηλοῦτον	(ἐδηλόετον)	ἐδηλοῦσθον	(ἐδηλόεσθον)
	3	ἐδηλούτην	(ἐδηλοέτην)	ἐδηλούσθην	(ἐδηλοέσθην)
P	1	ἐδηλοῦμεν	(ἐδηλόομεν)	ἐδηλούμεθα	(ἐδηλοόμεθα)
	2	ἐδηλοῦτε	(ἐδηλόετε)	ἐδηλοῦσθε	(ἐδηλόεσθε)
	3	ἐδήλουν	(ἐδήλοον)	ἐδηλοῦντο	(ἐδηλόοντο)

PRES INF δηλοῦν (δηλόειν)   δηλοῦσθαι (δηλόεσθαι)

PRES PART δηλῶν (δηλόων)   δηλούμενος (δηλοόμενος)

XIII. φημί

		Present			Imperfect
		IND	SUBJ	OPT	IMP	IND
S	1	φημί	φῶ	φαίην		ἔφην
	2	φῄς	φῇς	φαίης	φαθί or φάθι	ἔφησθα or ἔφης
	3	φησί	φῇ	φαίη	φάτω	ἔφη
D	2	φατόν	φῆτον		φάτον	ἔφατον
	3	φατόν	φῆτον		φάτων	ἐφάτην
P	1	φαμέν	φῶμεν	φαῖμεν or φαίημεν		ἔφαμεν
	2	φατέ	φῆτε	φαίητε	φάτε	ἔφατε
	3	φασί	φῶσι	φαῖεν or φαίησαν	φάντων	ἔφασαν

INF φάναι

PART: poetic φάς, φᾶσα, φάν (Attic prose φάσκων)

XIV. Dual of ἀγαθός and ὁ

	M	F	N	M	F	N
N, A, V	ἀγαθώ	ἀγαθά	ἀγαθώ	τώ	τώ	τώ
G, D	ἀγαθοῖν	ἀγαθαῖν	ἀγαθοῖν	τοῖν	τοῖν	τοῖν

XV.

οἶδα

	PERF IND	PLUPERFECT IND	PERF SUBJ
S 1	οἶδα	ᾔδη or ᾔδειν	εἰδῶ
S 2	οἶδας	ᾔδησθα or ᾔδεις	εἰδῇς
S 3	οἶδε (ν)	ᾔδει or ᾔδειν	εἰδῇ
D 2	ἴστον	ᾖστον	εἰδῆτον
D 3	ἴστον	ᾔστην	εἰδῆτον
P 1	ἴσμεν	ᾖσμεν or ᾔδεμεν	εἰδῶμεν
P 2	ἴστε	ᾖστε or ᾔδετε	εἰδῆτε
P 3	ἴσασι (ν)	ᾖσαν or ᾔδεσαν	εἰδῶσι (ν)

	PERF OPT	PERF IMPV
S 1	εἰδείην	
S 2	εἰδείης	ἴσθι
S 3	εἰδείη	ἴστω
D 2	εἰδεῖτον	ἴστον
D 3	εἰδείτην	ἴστων
P 1	εἰδεῖμεν or εἰδείημεν	
P 2	εἰδεῖτε or εἰδείητε	ἴστε
P 3	εἰδεῖεν or εἰδείησαν	ἴστων

PART εἰδώς (εἰδότος), εἰδυῖα (εἰδυίας), εἰδός (εἰδότος)

INF εἰδέναι

XVI.

ἡδύς

Singular

	Masculine	Feminine	Neuter
NOM	ἡδύς	ἡδεῖα	ἡδύ
GEN	ἡδέος	ἡδείας	ἡδέος
DAT	ἡδεῖ	ἡδείᾳ	ἡδεῖ
ACC	ἡδύν	ἡδεῖαν	ἡδύ
VOC	ἡδύ	ἡδεῖα	ἡδύ

Dual

	Masculine	Feminine	Neuter
N, A, V	ἡδεεῖ	ἡδεία	ἡδεῖ
G, D	ἡδέοιν	ἡδεάιν	ἡδέοιν

	Masculine	Plural Feminine	Neuter
N, V	ἡδεῖς	ἡδεῖαι	ἡδέα
GEN	ἡδέων	ἡδειῶν	ἡδέων
DAT	ἡδέσι (ν)	ἡδείαις	ἡδέσι (ν)
ACC	ἡδεῖς	ἡδείας	ἡδέα

XVII. Third Person Personal Pronoun

	Singular	Plural
NOM		σφεῖς
GEN	οὗ	σφῶν
DAT	οἷ	σφίσι (ν)
ACC	ἕ	σφᾶς

XVIII. Dual of πόλις and ἔθνος

N, A	πόλει	ἔθνει
G, D	πολέοιν	ἐθνοῖν

XIX. ἀλήθεια

	Singular	Dual	Plural
NOM	ἀλήθεια	ἀληθεία	ἀλήθειαι
GEN	ἀληθείας	ἀληθείαιν	ἀληθειῶν
DAT	ἀληθείᾳ	ἀληθείαιν	ἀληθείαις
ACC	ἀλήθειαν	ἀληθεία	ἀληθείας
VOC	ἀλήθεια	ἀληθεία	ἀλήθειαι

www.ingramcontent.com/pod-product-compliance
Lightning Source LLC
Chambersburg PA
CBHW080736300426
44114CB00019B/2616